The Art Of Attraction Marketing

Alex is an online marketing expert who has invested years into trying, testing, researching, mastering and proving successful online marketing strategies at intermediate and advanced levels.

This book is a Bible that all business owners should read and cherish. By implementing the strategies and techniques shared you can guarantee to see an increase in brand awareness, brand loyalty, sales frequency, value and volume.

Sales and Marketing is not part of your business, it is your business. The product and service is second to your sales and marketing as without customers, there is no business. Alex has clearly invested a lot of time into this book, and very few books have I seen which contain such valuable information.

Alex addresses many important frustratingly true points. Too many small minded business owners want the success of what big businesses do, whilst comparing their sales and marketing activities to small businesses.

To become a growing, successful company, you need to invest time and or money into sales and marketing. As Alex states throughout, it's all about a system any business can use to attract more customers and sales every day.

Danny Nevill, Managing Director, Universal Web Design

The Art Of Attraction Marketing

The proven formula to get new leads and customers every day

Alex Jenkins

Published by Leading Light Publishing

ISBN:
978-0993577413

DEDICATION

This book is dedicated to the most important person in my world, my best friend, my business partner, my mother, Alison Miles-Jenkins, who inspired me from an early age to break the norm and enter the world of business.

CONTENTS

THE BIG SHIFT

Our amazing online world has contributed significantly to the way we market and sell our products and services. This worked wonders for the early adopters, but now things are changing and marketing and selling are becoming much more challenging necessities of running a successful business.

However, without the right knowledge and skills, business owners think of them as necessary evils, because they don't understand how to do either effectively. As a result, potential customers, weary of their exposure to seeing promotional material everywhere online, now seem to have a built in sales radar: they will see your pitch coming from a million miles away.

It's ironic isn't it because people don't like to be sold to but there is no shortage of people wanting to buy stuff. The biggest question for you as a business owner though has to be this: Why, when they do want to buy, should they choose you and your stuff over everyone else?

Your business is competing in an environment where, unless you know exactly how to cut through the fog to grab attention and get your message across, your business will perish. This is why you must adopt the attraction marketing formula to make sure you not only get customers now but you create customers for life. This will increase the lifetime value of your customer tremendously and ultimately increase your profits.

It all starts with the relationship and not the initial sale. Think giving before taking. Your marketing messages don't want to be all about "buy my stuff" because 95% of people aren't even ready to "buy your stuff" at the moment they see those messages and before you know it they're gone forever and they're not coming back.

So against this highly competitive and challenging backdrop, can you imagine what it would mean to you to receive a never ending supply of leads and potential customers every day? How would that affect the success of your business?

Whilst the success of your business will rely on the never ending inward flow of leads and sales the initial hurdle to overcome is to first attract and capture a lead. The way that you do that is through a lead magnet that gets your prospects to put their hand up and say "yes I'm interested in what you have to offer". It's amazing because all of a sudden the relationship changes in your favour from that moment on. They've expressed interest in what you do and if you provide value through your lead magnet they'll be more open to your sales message.

If they don't buy from you right away don't panic: you still have something that's like gold dust. You have a lead that you can follow up through as many different offers as you like and you can continue to build and nurture the relationship. Your list of leads and customers that you continually attract and build will be an asset in your business that will ultimately give you the ability to create income at will.

This applies to any type of business. As long as you are a business owner, here is your continual challenge and goal: to attract leads, build a relationship, convert leads into customers for life and create income at will.

According to www.Bloomberg.com, 8 out of 10 small businesses fail. That's an amazing number! It doesn't seem fair does it? It's a harsh fact of life. Here's another one: most businesses simply don't have a clue about attraction marketing. They are way behind the game, with their mind-sets and belief systems rooted in outdated marketing and sales principles.

You don't need to be a part of that 80%. Most small businesses fail because of a lack of cash flow and without it your long term outlook isn't great. A recent study showed 87% of business owners struggle with cash flow, and nearly all of those businesses don't have systems in place to generate leads and clients. Cash is king as they say. So the key is to have a formula that'll generate leads and sales, constantly providing you with the cash flow you need.

I believe the art of attraction marketing is that formula and is the most critical skill you can learn to grow and build your business. Without it you'll forever be scratching around for work with no real idea where your next customer will come from. Who would want to live their business life like that?

To your success!

Alex Jenkins

CHAPTER 1:

GUESS WHAT?

YOU'RE IN THE MARKETING BUSINESS

Whatever business you are in these days you are most definitely in the marketing business. What this means is that you mustn't just be the expert in your product or service: you have to reinvent yourself and become an expert in marketing too.

When it comes to business, smart business owners are realizing this: they have to master the real world techniques of sales and marketing. You can have all the passion under the sun for what you do but if you can't sell or market it you will simply end up with nothing.

If you think about it selling impacts everyone, not just those of us in business. It's about influence and persuasion after all, isn't it? So your ability to sell or convince someone will ultimately affect key aspects of your life and your future. I truly believe that selling affects more than just business. What happens if you're trying to ask someone out on a date? You have to somehow sell yourself so that they get why they should agree to go out on a date. What about something as simple as getting people to like you or give you a job? Once again, your result will be based on your ability to market and sell yourself.

Look at any successful business owner, musician, pop star, sports person, celebrity and you'll see they're all exceptional at selling and marketing.

"Sales cures all" is the famous quote by Billionaire Mark Cuban.

No business owner can build a sustainable business without understanding sales and marketing and yet there are so many barriers that can get in the way. "Selling" has always had a bad name and, believe me, the rejection you experience when selling isn't for everyone.

My first taste of selling was going door to door trying to sell gas and electric when I was 18 and it was the worst experience of my life. Imagine a bitter day in January, in a poor, urban area, walking around in the freezing cold knocking on people's doors trying to convince them to switch energy suppliers. My pitch lasted about 5 seconds and soon was followed with a door slammed in my face.

I used to sit in the car, fuming with the frustration and humiliation of it all. I'm quite proud though to say I actually stuck it out for 4 months, and made 5 sales, which was an achievement considering I'd only received some really poor training. Can you imagine the sense of failure I felt?

I was determined never to feel like that again and took steps to ensure that I didn't. As my entrepreneurial journey blossomed I soon realized, thankfully, that selling wasn't about the "gift of the gab" but was actually about a certain language and formula that enabled you to influence someone.

That direct, hardcore selling approach just wasn't what I believed in and that's why I've taken the time and actions to master marketing that prequalifies and preconditions people to accept your sales message and that's exactly what this book is going to help you to do too. All of my marketing has been based on this "attraction" or "magnetic" method. It's a million miles away from pushing on people to get them to buy your product by literally shoving every product in their face until they finally buy something. You can do that of course, you can chase them down the street (some people actually do that don't they?), knock on doors, cold call on the phone, all of which are very uncomfortable.

As I've mentioned before getting a door slammed in your face constantly during a miserable January when you can't even feel your hands walking round the streets on a dark wet winter's night takes its toll on even the toughest of people. It's hard to pull off and it's uncomfortable for you and the potential customer. It actually puts people off buying and gives "selling" a bad reputation. And guess what? That feeling of rejection, one of things we humans fear so much, actually results in you falling out of love with what you're selling and you'll always end up scratching around for the next deal, in a business you're no longer passionate about.

Being in business and being successful involves many things. Some we'll discuss in this book, and others are outside its scope. One thing however is crucial. To weather the pressures, demands, disappointments and opportunities of being in business you have to be passionate about your product or service. It is that passion that will see you through and drive you on to learn all the amazing skills, know-how, short cuts, hacks and tips that can take you to the next level and beyond. Without these crucial 'must-haves', you are likely to get more of what you fear – rejection, and disappointment – and that can start a cycle that can bring you and your business down.

Take a look around you, at the businesses in your area, and at your competitors. You'll soon see that most of them are doing exactly what I've described. Naively, they are always pushing people to an offer and trying to get the initial sale. Customers really aren't going to be very receptive to it. If you resort to this too and for example you are spending money on online advertising, if you just promote the sale you'll be lucky to get a 1-2% conversion rate. That's not going to produce a very good return on investment. I'm sure that you really wouldn't want to do that, would you?

The one thing I learned very early on is that the money is in the relationship and value you provide to people, not in the initial sale. The best way to market to your potential customers is through "attraction" marketing to get people to raise their hand and say "yes I'm interested". You then have that lead that you can market to over and over again with different offers. To get people's attention and to get them to then put their hand up you'll need to be providing the right advertising message to them through paid media because there is no such thing as acquiring a lead or customer for free (that's the second thing I soon learned).

And here's the third insight I gained: your marketing is never a cost because it's an investment.

If, for every time you gave me £5 I gave you £25 back…how many £5 would you give me? As many as you could get your hands on, right? That's a 5 times return on investment. That's exactly how you have to look at your marketing. It's not a cost; it's an investment.

When you master your marketing you should expect to see a minimum of 5 times the return. Once you can achieve that you can really start scaling your business. But to do that you have to follow exact systems otherwise you'll burn through your marketing budget with little return and complain that "marketing doesn't work".

Marketing in the wrong hands is as lethal as putting all your money on lucky number 7! But I can tell you that if you become a smart business owner you'll master marketing and see some serious growth in your business. Never think that you can acquire a customer for free because it's not true and doesn't happen. In fact, chances are your first sale is the most unprofitable one you'll ever make but if you satisfy your customers, and deliver more than they ever thought they would get from you, then they will buy from you time and time again. That repeat purchasing concept is on every business owner's 'must-have' list and that's why the relationship counts and your thoughts should never be concentrated on just 'making a sale'. You'll always be spending money to acquire a customer and so that's why when you do get a new customer you want to keep them for as long as possible and get them to buy as frequently as possible. Remember this: it's always cheaper to keep a customer than to acquire a new one.

So it's now time to become an obsessive student of marketing. Marketing is so important to a business because you don't actually have a business until someone phones you up, walks through your door, orders your product online…you simply don't have a business without marketing.

The thing is that the endless amount of business development clutter everywhere actually makes it harder for you as a business owner to attract more customers through your door. Differentiation is what will help your business stand out from that clutter, with systems and processes that attract people to you as the preferred choice.

If you think about it a celebrity who turns up at a famous nightclub to do an appearance is likely being paid in the tens of thousands but the barman serving the drinks will be earning minimum wage. Why is that? Simply put, the barman is providing the deliverable...a drink....and there's millions that could perform the role effectively. However the celebrity is the person who actually attracts people and gets them through the door in the first place. That's a much taller order and few people would be able to do it. Think about your business; you don't want to be the one pouring drinks, you want to be the one who can attract customers, sell to those customers, get those customers to buy more, and then for those customers to multiply. You are now a student of marketing, you are in the marketing business and your attention should never stray far from it. It will provide you with the biggest compensation available as the money is truly in the marketing.

So you know that your success will rely on the constant never ending flow of leads and sales into your business. But how big will your flow be? If it's not big enough it becomes highly risky, so you need to create multiple sources from which you can flow leads and sales. And what kind of bait are you going to offer to attract your perfect customer?

Most businesses rely on one form of marketing. Take my mother's training and consultancy business. She had successfully run the business for 25 years with most years generating 6 figures revenue. What I soon learned was that she had for many years been operating the business purely from referrals and repeat business. She only had one source for her leads and sales. Her aim had not initially been to build a multimillion pound business as it had been in those days more of a lifestyle business to raise us three kids and give us the best start in life. I can happily say she delivered on that and she is an amazing mother.

When I joined the business I became obsessed with marketing, reading hundreds of books, attending courses, seminars, and mastermind groups, all to develop my understanding of marketing and sales. Literally tens of thousands has been invested in my education to learn this skill. But knowledge is worthless unless acted on so I started applying all the marketing strategies that I'd learnt and we started to see great results in our business.

We went from two sources to having over 10 ways to attract new leads and sales into our business. I quickly realised that marketing was my passion and that the skills, experience and knowledge I'd learnt could be used to help other people. That's when I started working with small businesses to help them transform their results.

I truly believe that if we'd just stuck to the two methods of referrals and repeat business we'd soon have been experiencing problems, but the biggest challenge for me was growth and scalability. You can't grow and scale a business relying on one or two sources of new customers. You're most likely only operating at 10% of your earning potential. The big shift for me was when I started exploring and testing multiple sources of marketing to bring us in more clients. But what I soon realised was that all these other sources were useless if you didn't have your positioning right, your website right, your follow up sequence right, your pitch right, your sales funnel right. The sources for new customers would be useless if this were the case. That's why I've given you a step by step formula for you to follow in this book so that you do everything right the first time.

Here are my top ten sources of marketing for leads and customers:

Google Adwords	Facebook
LinkedIn	Email Marketing
Webinars	Podcasts
Referrals	Networking
Direct Mail	Joint ventures

These marketing sources are where you go to find your ideal prospects and to then display a message that matches with your audience so that they take action. Through the formula I teach in this book you'll be able to use marketing sources that best suit your market. Unless your potential customers are in a professional type of role and are on LinkedIn it's useless to use that mechanism to attract leads, so you need to choose the sources that are relevant.

When it comes to your online and offline marketing you want to make sure everything fits together... It's like a puzzle. If you don't have all the pieces in the right place you can't finish the puzzle. There is no point writing a blog every week if you don't know how to optimise a blog so that it captures leads and converts buyers. It's just a waste of time... If you don't know how to drive traffic to your blog then no one is ever going to read it. Just like if you run a Pay Per Click (PPC) advertising campaign but don't have a good landing page, compelling copy, lead capture process, follow up process, then you're missing big parts of the puzzle and you'll struggle to get results. The good news is this book is a step by step formula so by the end of it you should have the puzzle completed.

I've not written this book to teach you everything there is to know about marketing and sales in general. I've crafted this book so that you, the smart business owner, can deploy proven and tested formulas that'll help you "attract" and generate leads and sales without actually working harder. You see the secret to smart marketing is to combine leading edge online and offline marketing that once tested can be left to run with very minimal effort. I'm talking about having other people maintaining these systems. This will mean that you can spend the time doing the things you want, that you are good at and which leverage your personal resources – knowledge, skills and abilities most effectively. With "attraction" marketing you concentrate on building a list of prospects. That's building a crucial asset base for your business. Remember, if you generate a lead and they don't buy, you can continue the relationship through email and direct mail. Not everyone will buy now so it's the relationship that counts.

I'm not going to be talking in this particular book about other very important areas of business such as mind-set, time management, leadership, etc. However I do highly suggest you take the time to study the mind-set of successful businesses owners. It's crucial as it completely changed my life when I realised that there was no "luck" to business. The best book, in my opinion, to get you started would be Napoleon Hill – 'Think and grow rich.' Why not read it after this one?

Most people put their stuff online or out to the world and just think people are magically going to turn up and buy it. I wish that were the case but's it's not. You can have people queuing up for your stuff. But it's not going to be down to magic or luck. It's going to be down to you applying, consistently, the right formula and system.

What this book will give you is a simple formula

for attracting the right kind of clients into your business and that'll reward you for years to come. This isn't a "rich quick" book or an offer of yet another new bright and shiny object. It's all about proven and tested strategies that'll allow you to scale and grow your business the smart way.

You can email me at success@smartbizsecrets.com

CHAPTER 2: THE FORMULA

The only thing that stands between making a sale and not, is a prospect's fear. They've been betrayed countless times in the past. They don't have confidence in others, they don't have confidence in themselves, and they don't want to be misled again. I'm guessing you can relate to that too. We've all been that prospect, haven't we?

The truth is unfortunately this: you've got so many negative factors as a marketeer business owner that are working against you from the word go. Add to this the fact that if you don't focus your marketing activity on lead generation you're leaving a bunch of money on the table.

Your business will not be controlled; instead you'll have what's known as random activity. Random activity is when you run marketing campaigns and hope that a number of people 'show up' – over the phone, by visiting your store, or by chance buy your product or service. It's not controlled and you'll only get interest from people who are ready to buy now. This is an important distinction. Your marketing shouldn't be random.   Instead it should be controlled. It should be based around capturing as many names, physical addresses, and email addresses as possible from people who are interested in what you can offer now and in the future. Then, through the right systems and processes, you build a relationship and gradually lower that sales resistance I mentioned before.

Applying the attraction marketing formula is the system that'll produce the right leads and customers into your business. When you apply this formula you'll attract people to you who have stepped forward, raised their hand, and have given you permission to communicate with them. It changes the whole process from trying to generate an immediate sale and being a pest to a welcomed guest. (There's some unintentional rhyming there. That's good as it's an easy way to remember that important point!)

When you attract a lead, normally you're exchanging a lead magnet in exchange for the person's contact information. Your lead magnet is something you give away for free as an ethical bribe to get people to put their hand up and say "Yes I want that". This is a lot different to trying to get people to buy now by using brute-force. So what you're actually doing is making the buying process less stressful for the prospect. You've given free information or a free trial. So they're going to be smarter and their sales resistance is going to be lower. All good news for you. A win/win for you both, in fact.

Your lead generation magnet is what will make people respond to your advertising and it's the bait that'll attract your ideal prospect and customer to your business. It has to be something that your target market wants, for which they are willing to step forward, raise their hand, give you their contact information and, most importantly, give you some level of permission to contact you.

Here is a list of alternative types of lead magnets you can offer for free to your prospects to get them to put their hand up and say that coveted "Yes I'm interested" sentence:

Webinar

DVD

Products (For example complementary items to your main offering. An example would be if you sell suits you could offer free ties or cuff links)

CD

White papers

Trial

Guide

Case Study

Taster Session

Coupon

Newsletter

Demonstration

Tool Kit

Templates

Package

Consultation

Prize draw

Survey

Discount

Training session

Consumer awareness guide

So you can see there is a huge range of possibilities to offer. Remember, a lead magnet is the attraction bait to get people to step forward.

For our training and consulting business, one of our lead magnets for a complaints handling training course is a report called. "Why are you getting so many complaints? How to reduce complaints and resolve the situation". It's all about sending your prospect cool stuff that can make them more educated, help them resolve a challenge or meet a pressing need. This means you've flipped the situation from looking like another business trying to sell them something into a business that is actually helping them. However most people go wrong at this stage because they forget that they're not actually selling anything at this point. You're only sending a lead magnet and it's the start of a whole process. You're not one-shot selling. Anything else you do at this stage gets in the way. Equally, don't get carried away at this stage and give so much for free that they will never need any help or other products from you again. I've seen many businesses make this mistake, too.

I want to remind you of a point I stressed earlier about assets. Generating leads is more crucial than you might at first think because your leads and customers become your list and the biggest asset you can ever have in your business is a list. Your list is the mechanism you use to develop your relationship with your prospects and customers. When you build a list of prospects and customers it gives you the ability to create income on demand. I can tell you now that the most successful business owners have hundreds of thousands of people on a list that at the click of an email can generate a surge of sales for their business and a huge boost to the bank account. Just imagine that. You can build that too, over time.

Once you've generated a lead the follow up process starts and the next step in the system begins. Through the follow up process you continue to build the relationship and take the next step in your sales process. Now your sales process will determine what happens in the follow up process. For example, you may have decided in advance that the next step might be to arrange a free, short consultation, organise a valuation, a presentation, an appointment, demonstration, or even a low-level/low-ticket sale but don't get too ahead of yourself at this point.

As we go through the book I uncover each part of the formula step by step but for now here's a visual diagram of how the attraction marketing formula works in its most basic form. There are more elements to the system that I reveal later but as a basic understanding you can break it down to three main parts. You have to first send traffic to your lead magnet, the lead magnet works as bait to capture people's information, then once you have their information you follow up according to your sale process.

To add to the formula I want to mention the marketing triangle that my mentor Dan Kennedy uses as it's very important. Kennedy says that the right way to create a powerful marketing campaign is to have three main components work together.

Message: What do we say?

Market: Who are we saying it to?

Media: How do we take the message and deliver it to the person it's intended for?

It's very important to have all three components

work together to create a powerful marketing campaign. If one fails your marketing will fail. Dan talks about a three-legged stool. If any leg is too short it's hard to balance a glass of water on it or sit on it. If you miss a whole leg, the stool won't work at all. All three have to fit together in a way that's effective.

Where most businesses go wrong when it comes to marketing is fundamentally:

Wrong Message

Wrong Market

Wrong Media

If you get one wrong the rest of them won't work.

So, when you think about your message you need to keep in mind the following series of key questions:

Have you outlined the benefits of your product or service matched to their problems?

Is your message clear and interesting?

Have you connected with your ideal customer's problems and what they want to achieve?

What do they need and how can you help them?

When you think about your market you need to know exactly who it is you're targeting.

Keep in mind the following key things:

Who is your perfect customer and what is their customer avatar?

Where are they from?

Where do they "hang out"?

What gender are they?

How old are they?

What's their ethnicity?

What's their marital status?

What's their educational background?

What religion do they follow?

Which political party do they support?

Where do they work?

Do they have children?

What are they passionate about?

Brainstorm your perfect customer answering all of the questions above and more. Find out what their pain points and difficulties are. Why are you the right business to solve their problems?

Moving on, when you think about your media you need to keep in mind the following key question:

How are you going to deliver your message?

Media is the platform you send traffic from. If you

don't know what media your potential customers are hanging out on you won't marry up your market and media. So if you're targeting people over 70, then Facebook advertising probably won't be the best choice! With the power of digital marketing now a lot of business owners forget about more traditional forms of media, such as direct mail. The truth is you need a mix and you want to use whatever media fits best for your target market. So which media platform suits your message and market? How do you know? Have you researched it? Do you need to check again?

Here's a few examples of media you can buy advertising from:

Facebook

LinkedIn

Twitter

Google

Yahoo

YouTube

Instagram

Display networks

Physical sales letters

Print adverts

Shock and awe boxes

Radio

Billboards

To get the most out of your marketing you'll want to use a mixture of online and offline media to maximise your chance of receiving a response. Why would you want to limit the success of your results by putting all of your eggs in one basket? In the earlier chapter I demonstrated to you how important it is to have multiple ways to generate leads and new customers. The key to success with paid advertising especially is to know exactly what your results are. This is through tracking and measuring your campaigns. If you don't know what your results are you'll be at risk of wasting your money.

CHAPTER 3: WHY YOU?

"The way you position yourself and your compelling reason for why someone should do business with you will ultimately reflect your success" - Alex Jenkins

Remember, your business is competing in an environment where you have to cut through the fog to get attention and get your message across or your business will perish. It's that simple.

If you think about it why should your customers do business with you? What's unique and special about your business? If you can't think of a big enough reason for why people should do business with you then you'll find it extremely hard to sell them your product or service. I truly believe before you can even think about your "why" you have to be totally sold yourself on your product or service. Be 100% confident that what you can deliver is the best.

At the time of writing this book Donald Trump is currently running for President of the United States and he comes to mind when I think about being confident in what you can deliver being the best. Love him or hate him he's accomplished some amazing things in his life and for that I respect him. It's also good to take note of what a Billionaire does and says. Here's Donald Trump in his own words about confidence and greatness...

"People may not always think big themselves but they get very excited by those who do. People want to believe something is the biggest and the greatest and the most spectacular. Some people have written I'm boastful, but they are missing the point. If you're devoting your life to creating a body of work and you believe in what you do, and what you do is excellent, you'd damn well better tell people you think so. Subtlety and modesty are appropriate for nuns, but if you're in business, you'd better learn to speak up and announce your significant accomplishments to the world"

The long and the short of it is you must believe in yourself and get completely sold on the fact that you're the best!

Before you can even begin to start working on your website, ordering stock, fitting out an office or shop, getting business cards printed etc you need to stop! You need to stop and think about how you're going to position yourself and your business against all the competition out there. You'll be wasting your time and money getting business cards printed if you're not going to include your Unique Selling

Point (USP) or a couple of sentences that'll grab someone's attention. "Joe Bloggs" - financial advisor - Call 0800 000 000 - www.joebloggs.com isn't going to cut it quite frankly.

Remember you want to be running a smart business not a stupid one and the biggest mistake of them all is to rush into things without even thinking of your positioning and USP. You can't be like everyone else; you've got to stand out if you want to get ahead because if you can't clearly articulate what makes your business unique, how can you expect anyone else to care?

Once you're completely sold on your product or service you need to decide on your "why" and use that in your marketing material and sales pitch. The other term for your "why" is your USP. A lot of people struggle with this one from my experience. When you think about your USP you need to think about what's special about your product or service. Discovering your USP is not an easy task but you must create one for your product or service. Too many companies are just trying to be "me-too" companies.

However, you cannot be just like the next guy and expect to make a profit in a global economy. With the rise in competition it's just too easy for people to go to another shop, another website, another restaurant, another hotel. There are just too many choices so you need to stand out from the rest if you want to succeed. You need uniqueness to your product, service, or offer. What can you offer that no one else can? Can you offer the best guarantee, better service, free technical support and maintenance, free shipping, faster shipping, faster turnaround time? Think of something that will set you apart from all your competitors and make sure you tell them you're the best. It also allows you to command higher prices with price elasticity.

The best USP should try and be something that's at least aligned to your target market. Simply stating you deliver the best service or you're the 'number one' isn't going to cut it. Not everyone will believe that you're 'number one' or will actually care if you are but to some people it will matter. What you have to do is to tailor it, make it specific, relevant and meaningful to your target market. And remember that customer avatar. That gives clarity. Some people like to make up a 'photo fit' type of image of their ideal customer avatar and have it in front of them when they are working; they find this gives more clarity and so helps to keep them on track when working out these kinds of strategic marketing challenges. You could do this too.

Coming up with your USP seems like a very hard task but you can start with your positioning in terms of how you are different to all your competition. So make sure you spend time researching. You've probably heard of the old adage "To fail to prepare is to prepare to fail" and nowhere is that more true than with this.

Another way you could look at your USP is speed, if that could be relevant. A great example is the USP FedEx used to use that combines the essence of speed.

"When it absolutely, positively has to be there overnight."

You can see how they guarantee that it will deliver their packages safely and on time. It delivers the benefits of what they do. It's market focused and extremely powerful. It's a differentiator. It's memorable. So another way to create your USP is to guarantee something. FedEx made a guarantee that you'll get the package overnight. How could you guarantee an outcome for your target market? Think about how it's going to grab people's attention, stop them in their tracks and take some kind of action. Think about your customers' wants and desires, not their needs. With the FedEx example people just want it the next day, they don't usually need it the next day. Wants usually override needs emotionally and in marketing. So that's exactly what their USP delivered on. When you come up with a few ideas for your USP just think about it for a while, run it past people, and get feedback. Will it be remembered by your customers or not? Once you've decided on your USP make sure you tell everyone about it over and over again so everyone knows exactly what sets you apart from the rest. Shout it from the rooftops.

The right USP is essential for your business to

get attention with all the millions of other businesses over the world. The rest of your marketing should then be built around your USP.

The Expert Positioning Secret

As positioning is a big part of your USP, if you're in a service based business here's a big secret. It'll allow you to command your prices and have less sales resistance. It's all about becoming an expert. Now I'm not talking about being a professor or a scientist, I'm talking about someone who really knows their stuff when it comes to their particular niche. If you run a landscaping business you want to be positioned as the expert not just another gardener. The expert can command higher prices because of their positioning. Even if you sell products you should still try and create some kind of expert status. You'll have more value in your industry and therefore be commanding more money. Being an expert will also help you with your argument for "why" people should do business with you.

Here are some big reasons why you should position yourself as an expert:

Command higher prices

People will pay more to have an expert just based on the psychological effect it creates. Think about this with doctors, specialists and consultants, for example.

People Come To You

When you're an expert people will come and find you.

Be The Leader

You'll be seen as a leader in your space and opportunities will open up to you.

Lowers Sales Resistance

When you're seen as an expert, you'll find it's easier to sell to people.

I could write a whole book about establishing an expert status but this book is about a formula you can use to generate more leads and sales into your business. If positioning yourself as an expert is suitable then I'd highly recommend it.

Here are a few ways you can position yourself as an expert in your industry:

Write a book

Publish articles

Host a podcast

Online video show

Webinars

Claim your position in your industry

Limit access to you

Raise your prices

Speak at events

Write a monthly newsletter

Be featured on TV

Be featured on radio

Write a blog

Having an expert status will really add to your "why" and positioning in the market place. It's also easier to use "attraction" marketing if you're an expert in your industry. So this strategy wins on all fronts doesn't it?

Now you should realise how important your USP and reason "why" is to your business. It's the foundation for the rest of this book and you shouldn't move on to the next chapter until you've at least identified something that'll make you unique and different from the rest. Remember you can't just say you're the best, or you give the best service. Try and relate that into something that's specific to your target market.

Here's what you want to consider when coming up with your USP:

What's the best thing you do?

How can people benefit from it?

Identify the people you're targeting

Can you fill a gap in the market?

Will someone remember it and spark interest?

Is it believable or full of BS?

What's the biggest problem you can solve?

Can you offer speed?

A big guarantee

The experience you provide

Price advantage

Promise

Niche

CHAPTER 4: KNOW YOUR CUSTOMER

When it comes to your marketing it's always very easy to try and attract everyone. In fact, it's almost irresistible to do this. You always want a bigger piece of the pie and it's very easy to try and attract "everyone". Businesses often get a sense of reassurance if they are throwing out their net as widely as possible.

That's what the big companies can do and you may be tempted to do it but they've got very different agendas and very big pockets! When you think about the message or advertising you want to display you need to be specific. You must know who it is that you're targeting and where it is they "hang out". Think of it as an inverted funnel; you want to start out small with a specific message to a specific audience then grow out as you start to scale your business. My point is you want to know exactly who it is you're trying to attract to your website or offer. The reason for this is so that you can figure out where it is they are. Once you've figured out where they are you can put your message in front of them via online or offline marketing channels. If not then the person that sees your message will not match and therefore take no action. So success with this sounds simple doesn't it? In theory it is. In practice it's so much harder.

Your potential customers all hang out in similar places so wouldn't it make sense to find them and target them with a specific message that resonates with them, calls them out, and makes them takes action?

How you can burn through your marketing budget extremely quickly is by not knowing who your target market is and instead casting a very wide net with your message. This is by far the biggest mistake I see most business owners make with their marketing and leads to them being very sceptical about spending money to attract customers.

If you were going to knock on doors in your area and you wanted to sell boiler replacements you could knock on every door couldn't you? But what if you could knew ahead of time that there was one house in your area where the boiler kept breaking down on the coldest of winter nights, it was on its last legs and the homeowners had to keep calling out plumbers to get it going again. They kept getting told by plumbers that they needed a new one soon but didn't do anything about it. Would you want to knock on that door or hope that you came across it? Would you want to knock on all the other doors in the area and waste your time? That's what targeting is all about; you want to put the right message in front of the right people.

The first part to understanding who your customer is, is to be really specific, to really know your customer inside and out. You want to know what makes them tick and what they really care about. What pain points do they have that you're able to solve? What do they desire? Are they searching for what you can solve right this second?

You even want to be as specific as age, gender, hobbies, personality, interests, values, income range, religion, married, divorced, etc. This is so that you can target with laser precision to get the best results from your marketing. The beauty of targeting people precisely is that you only do business with people you can actually help. You're in the driver's seat if you like which will ultimately make your life better. You're not chasing every customer, you know exactly who you want to work with and the type of people you want to buy your product or service. Trying to get people from a position of desperation is very ugly and will leave you constantly worrying where your next customer will come from. This formula I'm teaching though this book will actually put you in a position where you can do business with people you actually like.

Once you know exactly the type of customer you want to attract, you'll then need to know where that customer is. The reason you need to find them is simple…traffic. The word traffic means sending people i.e. "traffic" to your offer. Online traffic examples are websites, social media, search engines, YouTube…whereever your customers are hanging out. Offline traffic examples are direct mail, magazines, newspapers, print, door to door, people passing your store. So finding out first where your customers are needs some serious research.

It's not as complicated as you might think though... The best place to start is Google seeing as it's the biggest search engine in the world and Google will actually tell you what people are searching for every day. In Chapter 8 on traffic sources I go into detail about using Google as a traffic source but just to give you an idea of how you can use Google as a research tool, you'll want to sign up to Google Adwords and use the keyword planner tool to research keywords related to your market. Google will tell you how many times your specific keyword is searched a month.

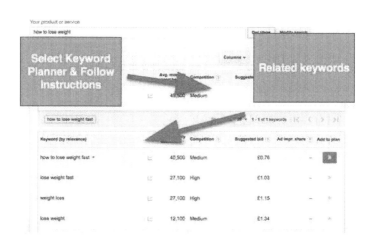

So, by using Google's keyword planner you can uncover what people are actually searching for. As we are on the topic of losing weight with this particular screenshot example I will do the next example for a personal trainer. So if I were a personal trainer searching for where my potential customers could be I'd start with Google and do a search for my local area.

Ad group ideas	Keyword ideas			Columns ▼		
Search terms			**Avg. monthly searches** ?	**Competition** ?	**Suggested bid** ?	**Ad**
personal trainer london		⊯	2,400	High	£4.16	

Show rows: 30 ▼ 1 - 1 of 1 keyword

Keyword (by relevance)		**Avg. monthly searches** ?	**Competition** ?	**Suggested bid** ?	**Ad**
personal training london	⊯	880	High	£5.45	
london personal trainer	⊯	320	High	£4.43	
personal trainer in london	⊯	140	High	£3.74	
personal trainer north london	⊯	170	High	£3.16	

So you can see in the screenshot that the keyword "personal trainer London" gets searched 2,400 times. So the answer to the question 'are my potential customers on Google?' would be yes for this example. They're actively searching for what you do every single month. Imagine if using my formula you were able to convert just 5 new clients a month from Google alone, what impact would that have to your business? I know that for our training consultancy 5 new clients a month from Google would bring in at least £10,000 a month! It's super exciting but don't dive into anything yet as I'll show you how to use Google to drive traffic in Chapter 8. Just start playing around with the keyword tool and see what other keywords match your business that you maybe didn't think your target market would search for.

What about Facebook? Facebook's more than 1.44 billion monthly active users around the world spend an average of 20+ minutes per day on the social network, liking, commenting, and scrolling through status updates, according to analysts from Needham, citing comScore data. I'm pretty sure that your potential customers are active on Facebook right now. Did you know that at the time of writing this book Facebook is worth $46 Billion and did you know how they make money? From people like you and me...advertising. So why is that a good thing? Well, that means Facebook wants to work with us to make it as easy as possible for us to target our potential customers because if we get good results they'll also profit in return. We can display adverts right in people's news feeds based on many different targeting factors. You'll want to check out Facebook to find groups related to your target market. Which pages are related to your market that people like? Do some digging around to see where your potential customers are hanging out on Facebook.

It's exciting isn't it to know that your customers are out there right now just waiting for you to deliver the right message and right bait in front of them? Imagine you're a miner looking for gold. You start researching the area, planning where you're going to dig, you start prodding and trying to find where the gold is. Based on your research you know that there is gold on that ground but you're not sure where it is. You continue to dig and all of a sudden you find a bit of gold. Gold normally forms in pay streaks, so you dig deeper and deeper until you find a pay streak. It pays to do the research because if you can find where your target market is then the gold is there.

If you sell Business to Business (B2B) then it's highly likely that your potential customers have LinkedIn profiles. Take a look to find out which groups they're in. Start looking at all platforms online and if you know that a particular website attracts your target market you'll want to reach out and come to some kind of Joint Venture (JV) deal or list renting arrangement with the owner.

You can also use Twitter very effectively if you don't have much of a marketing budget and you're targeting B2B. This is how I started to attract our customers through Twitter in the early days. You see most people like to show off in their profile about what it is they do especially if they use their profile to promote themselves. This is great for anyone with a limited marketing budget because you can find these people very easily with a simple tool. This simple tool is called Tweet Adder and I'm sure there is now additional software. I used Tweet Adder a long time ago and our marketing has come a long way since then but if your target market is on

Twitter then it's a cost effective way of connecting with them. So you'll want to use Tweet Adder or similar software and search for keywords in people's bios. For example if your target market is training directors you would put that keyword in, set the location and the software will display every profile in that area that had your keyword in it. You'll then know that your target market is on Twitter and it's another goldmine you can tap into. Once you get your search results back you can add them to a Twitter list. Twitter lists are made within your profile and you can then go back to that list to connect with people. I had great success with this and got a lot of new clients. I managed to get a meeting with a major high street retailer and a global delivery service and close both clients. It's quite time intensive and if you have members of staff you can outsource the backroom social media work to them to do.

Trade magazines are great. If you know your potential customers read them then it's a perfect source of leads and you'll want to look to using that as a source for advertising, or if you have established yourself as an expert in a niche, then contact a journalist and get your articles in the magazine. My mother did this very effectively within a niche market and became sought-after very quickly for articles. She wrote for lots of professional magazines and then that led to speaking engagements within the profession and the respective trade associations. Your message has to match with your market to get any kind of response, though and that's why it's extremely important to do good research on where your potential customers hang out. Imagine you're at a football match and you stood outside the away fans seating area trying to sell the home team's shirt. Do you think you'd sell any shirts? The obvious answer is no, they don't support the home team and so your message to market match is completely wrong. You would be targeting the wrong people so you're not going to sell anything. It sounds very simple but you'd be amazed by the amount of businesses that don't spend enough time finding their customers and finding where they hang out. Now if you move your shirt selling stool to the other side of the football ground where the home team supporters are walking past in their hundreds you've now got a hot market to sell to.

I've always been a fan of the UK Apprentice which is hosted by Sir Alan Sugar. For those of you who don't know Sir Alan Sugar, he was brought up on a council estate in London and went from nothing to being worth hundreds of millions of pounds. If you've not read his book "What you see is what you get" I'd highly recommend it. I can remember being on holiday reading his book and I didn't leave the sun lounger every day until evening. I was completely captivated and engrossed in it. I'm quite a slow reader and I like to take my time but at the end of the 10 days I'd finished it and arrived back in the UK a completely different person. I now read every single night because the impact a book can have on you is simply amazing. If you have not yet read Sir Alan Sugar's book you must read it! The aim of the Apprentice is that Sir Alan Sugar sets tasks every week and the team that gets the most sales wins, and from the losing team one person is fired. I love watching it to pick up on the mistakes that they make and one key mistake that often comes to mind is all about having the right market to sell to. The aim of one particular task on a recent episode of the programme was to make and sell a real ale beer. The team with the most sales at the end of the day won. Now for those who don't know, real ale beer is popular with older men from my understanding. So where would real ale drinkers congregate? It's not a hard one to figure out...a real ale festival and that's exactly what one team did. They set up a stool at a real ale festival where their target market was and had the best chance of making the most sales. Their message to market match was spot on. The other team on the other hand opted to set up shop in a beer garden of a local pub. Common sense can tell you that just because it's a beer garden of a local pub does not mean it's going to be filled with real ale drinkers. What made it even worse was there wasn't actually anyone in the beer garden...a complete disaster. They failed to identify where their target market would be and lost the task. An important thing to remember is they could have had the best tasting real ale in the world but the best real ale in the world won't sell if you don't put it in front of the right people. Take some time now to work out where your potential customers are hanging out and congregating. Remember it's like digging for gold, and so when you find them and put the right message in front of them, they'll reward you with sales.

When I joined the family business and I started applying all the marketing knowledge I'd been studying from my mentors I soon realised that we had a fundamental flaw in our marketing and the way we communicated to our market. When I first started thinking about changing our messaging I realised that most of our marketing material was speaking to the person that would be actually sitting on our training courses, completing the learning. So the person that we were targeting was an individual in a company who would be attending our courses. But the person who was actually buying our courses wasn't the person that sat on our training courses. The decision maker and the person actually giving us the work was the HR Manager or Director. I knew straight away that our target marketing had been all over the place. Our messaging didn't speak directly to the target market we actually needed to attract. From that point on I made sure that every piece of marketing was directed at the people actually buying from us and not just attending the course.

When you know who your customers are and you use attraction marketing, an added benefit is that you'll actually find that people find you through your business's reputation. So go out there and find the gold!

CHAPTER 5: FOCUS ON THE RELATIONSHIP NOT THE INITIAL SALE

This point may well surprise you: the first sale you make is the most unprofitable and hardest you'll ever make. However the good news is that if you satisfy your customers, and deliver more than they ever thought they would get from you they will buy from you time and time again. Most businesses don't do this. It's so rare, and yet so profitable and that's why the relationship counts and your thoughts should never be concentrated on just making a sale. The money is in the relationship you make not the direct sale and that's why building a great relationship from the very start is so important. As I've said, people have had enough of "buy my stuff now". They are more discerning. They want to know, like, and trust you before they decide to buy from you and if you do it right they will be fans of you and your business for life. People are so much more connected today and authenticity is really important. This in retrospect is a side effect of our super connected world and that's why in most cases the traditional old way of selling to get people to buy now doesn't work very well anymore. The entire way of selling, if you think about it, has undergone quite a transformation and I can see this even when I look back over the last few years. Back when I started selling our corporate training courses I didn't have a clue about attraction marketing and building a relationship before asking for the sale. I'd cold call potential prospects and I'd actually be in a queue waiting for the person before me to finish their pitch. As you can imagine my pitch wasn't welcomed. I knew I had to find a different way to get people to buy our courses. That's when I started focusing on building a relationship and not trying to pitch people for the initial sale.

The First Date

Imagine you've been single for a couple of years and you've decided you've had enough of the late night partying lifestyle and you're ready to settle down into a serious relationship. Every time you see your best friend you keep on complaining about being single and how you're looking to settle down. So just by chance your friend has a new colleague at work and she's single, meets all your criteria and is just your type. You start getting excited when he starts describing how she looks, what she's into, and how she loves dogs, just like you. Just by chance she's also single looking to settle down with someone. You ask your friend to set up a blind date and she accepts. You get all excited and even go out and buy a complete set of new clothes for the blind date. As you approach the coffee shop where you've agreed to meet you can feel your hands getting all sweaty as you're turning the steering wheel and parking your car. Your heart rate increases, anxiety levels go up, this could be the one, and everything you've heard about her is true. She's amazing. You can see she's standing outside waiting for you, so you walk right up to her and say "Will you marry me"? The poor woman is in complete shock, the answer of course is an emphatic 'NO' and before you can even say another word she's running down the street calling for help. Now this example might seem a bit drastic and unrealistic but when you relate this to business it's not. The moral of the story is 'don't propose on the first date'! Yet so many businesses are saying "buy my stuff, buy my stuff" with no thought or consideration for what it is they're doing and how it makes people feel. In fact it alienates people, they don't want to hear another "buy my stuff" pitch from another sales person. And the fact of the matter is asking for the sale has a lower response rate because only people who are ready to buy right now will take you up on your offer anyway. One example of direct selling is doing cold calling the wrong way. I say the wrong way because if you do it the right way it can be very effective; buying an email list and the first email you send out is a sales pitch is another. Put yourself in the prospect's shoes for a moment. That's actually always a good thing to do. They don't know you, they don't know if you're reliable, they don't know if your product works, they don't know if you can achieve results for them. They don't really know anything about you or your business so why would they even consider buying anything at all from you? It's crazy to think you can just pitch people to "buy my stuff now" but this approach has been going on for years. It's also very dumb to just put something out there and pray that people will think it's so amazing that they'll buy it then and there. Do you want to run a successful business for the next 5, 10, 20 years? Well then you better start thinking about relationship marketing not direct selling. Building profitable relationships is the key to making sure you're still around in a years' time let alone 10. That's why in this book I'm showing you how to attract the right kind of customer into your business and keep them for as long as possible.

The way customers gather information about businesses and make decisions has changed. People's time and attention is very scarce and their suspicion to marketing and direct selling is on high alert. Why should they trust and like you over all the competition out there? If you just ask them to buy straight away they're not going to feel valued.

Build a lasting relationship with your customers. I can tell you that in our consulting business we've had clients for 20 years who've annually spent £10,000+ because we've always focused on the relationship and not the sale. We always deliver more than our clients can ever imagine and they reward us with repeat business for years. Imagine if we'd just concentrated on the initial sale and didn't build a relationship, we'd have lost hundreds of thousands! Imagine if we'd just pitched up saying "buy my stuff now" we wouldn't have even made the initial sale in the first place because people only do business with people they like and trust.

Every consumer has one question at the back of their mind and that is 'who can I trust?' Believe it or not this question is always at the back of their minds whether they themselves know it or not. We now live in a society where trust is a very big thing. Every business in the world is in the people business - the solving of people's problems is what we do. If your carpet is dirty then you have a problem and you need a vacuum to clean up the mess. If you've got lower back pain you've got a problem and you need a chiropractor to adjust you. If your staff don't know how to chair meetings that are effective you've got a problem and you need an expert to train your staff. If you think about your business it's likely you are solving some sort of problem someone is facing. So therefore we are dealing with people, we are in the people business and people have to know, like, and trust someone before they exchange money to solve that problem. When I think about trust and value I think of the Wolf of Wall Street film that was based on the life of Jordan Belfort. The film portrayed someone who had fantastic skills, and was a real expert at selling but had no interest at all in building value or a relationship with his customers. The film showed him chasing the money...MONEY. MONEY. MONEY and that initial first sale. It appeared he had no focus on actually helping people put their money into good investments, he didn't seem to care about if what he was doing was legal or not We saw examples in the film where people lost their life savings overnight and ultimately it was his downfall.

Every industry has scammers and people who are not ethical and at the end of the day for them it comes down to chasing the money and the sale not the relationship. If you chase the initial sale, you risk not seeing that customer ever again. All of this adds to the number of people walking around with this anti sales barrier, a preconceived risk factor attached to every decision they make that involves a transaction of money.

Removing the fear people have through your marketing and building a long lasting relationship is the key. The aim of attraction marketing is to remove people's fear before you actually ask them to buy anything. As a business owner and marketeer you need to remove the fear so when that when the time is right people will be more open to your sales message. So many of your potential customers are bombarded with endless offers from your competitors. Building trust and a relationship will make you stand out from the rest.

With the attraction marketing formula that you'll use, the process of turning a prospect into a customer is based on an ongoing relationship that will make you stand out in the market place.

Your Biggest Asset

So, bearing all this in mind, the biggest asset you can ever have in your business is a list. Your list is the mechanism you use to develop your relationship with your prospects and customers. When you build a list of prospects and customers it gives you the ability to create income on demand. I can tell you now that the most successful business owners have hundreds of thousands of people on a list that at the click of an email can generate a surge of sales for their business.

Your list is the record of leads and customers you have that enables you to market to them over and over again. Please note that 'market to over and over again' are the keywords here. Imagine if with every new customer you got you weren't allowed to keep any of their details! This would be like suicide because if you remember earlier on I told you that the most unprofitable sale you'll ever make is the first. Why? Because most of the profit you'll ever make is from your customers buying from you again and again. And the way you get customers to buy over and over again is to continue the relationship and market to them through your list.

The two core types of lists are online and offline. Your online list is your email database and offline is your direct mail list. Both give you the ability to send an offer via email or direct mail. Your list can be made up of leads and customers. You'll want, however, to segment the two as you'll have different offers and messages. In the next chapter you'll find out how you attract leads and build your list.

The size of your list doesn't matter, it's how you market to your list through specific marketing campaigns that'll allow you to create income on demand. In our training business December was always a quiet month for us as most companies were winding down ready for the new year and developing their staff was not top on the agenda. I'd managed to grow our list to roughly 1200 people at that point and I knew through our list we could generate more sales. I can remember my mum saying 'it's almost Christmas time Alex, start thinking about winding down, we can make a big push for it in the New Year'. But I knew I had a list of 1200 people who already knew, liked, and trusted our business. I knew that if I created the right kind of offer I could go into the New Year with a load of new bookings.

So I took pen to paper and mapped out a four part email campaign and a 3 part direct mail campaign with an irresistible offer. This offer was so good that my prospects and clients were sure to fall right back in their chair when they read it. When you write sales copy you want to be having that kind of effect on people. The words that you write have a serious effect on your bottom line. One of the greatest copywriting legends that ever lived, Gary Halbert, once said that when you write sales copy you want to write it like you've got a gun to your head. That's how important sales copy is to your business and it's a skill that is learnt. So armed with my words of wisdom from Gary Halbert I sat in my office imagining I had a gun to my head as I started writing the offer. I knew it had to be one of the best sales letters I'd ever written because our target market just didn't really buy at that time of the year. I thought long and hard about the offer and I decided to run a very special discount of 50% OFF but only on courses and coaching booked within 7 days of the offer. Armed with my knowledge of direct response marketing I limited it to only 10 people as well to create scarcity. You'll find out that I'm not a big fan of discounting fees and competing on price but in this instance I knew I had to have an offer so good that people couldn't say no. We'd never run a discount like this before so as you can imagine the response was overwhelming. Not only did we generate £11,250 in initial sales, we reactivated clients who hadn't used us in a few years who then went on to book more work through the year. Can you imagine if I'd sent that offer out to people completely cold that didn't know, like, and trust our business? I'd have never got that kind of response because people would have been tuned into their sales radar. But because we'd manufactured a relationship with people on our list they were more open to an offer and their sales resistance was a lot lower. That's why your list is your asset and why it's extremely important to build a relationship from the start that continues for years. In return you can use your list to create income on demand.

Social Media lists

Email and direct mail lists will always be the best way to communicate with your prospects and customers but social media is now playing a significant role. Social media has allowed people to create a relationship and a following of hundreds of thousands of people who closely follow every move they make. This is relationship marketing at its best and the smart ones know that they need to take their social media followers and get them into an email list where they can control the process better. The thing is people don't follow brands, and they don't follow businesses. They do follow people and characters. Why do you think that big companies hire in celebrities and make up characters who they promote on their TV commercial? People want to connect with people. Social media is also the perfect platform to keep the ongoing relationship with your prospects and customers. The biggest of all is YouTube where people can really get to know, like and trust you. If you're not using YouTube in your business it's probably going to be one of the biggest breakthroughs you can make. Video is on the rise and it's likely it will take over everything. The average user on YouTube spends 40 minutes at a time. It's the perfect platform for people to really follow you and develop a deep relationship with you. It's also a great platform for generating leads.

Here's some examples of people building a following and crushing it on YouTube:

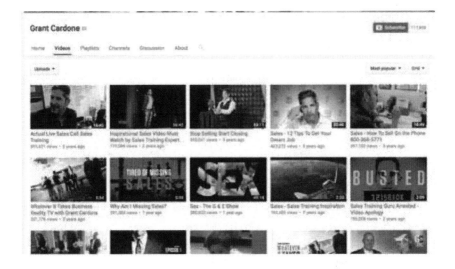

I've been following Grant Cardone for a number of years now and he's one of my mentors. Grant is an amazing example of expert content marketing and building a relationship through YouTube.

He's building value every day and I'd watched a number of videos before I even bought any of his books or products.

I felt like I knew him and could trust him even before I saw something from him that pitched one of his products. He has over 2,000 videos and 117,808 subscribers. Every time he releases a new video I always try to find time to watch it because he makes me feel like I know him and I can trust him.

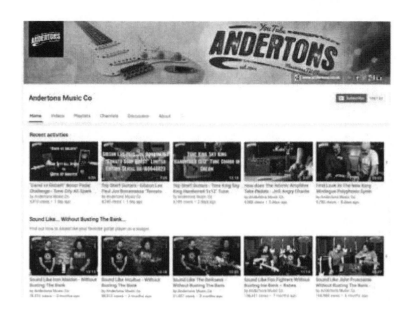

Andertons music store is another great example of using YouTube to develop a relationship. Music is my passion, I've been a drummer since the age of 7 and have been playing the guitar since I was 16. So when I was looking for a new guitar I shopped around a bit on Google but didn't have much luck. I came across Andertons who had the guitar I wanted but here's how they were different. Instead of just a product page like everyone else they had a video review of the guitar on the product page. I could watch a professional play the guitar in different styles, reviewing it for me before I bought it. After watching that one video I decided to check their channel out and watch many, many more. In fact I spent much of the evening going through their videos. I felt like I knew the guys on there, I had a relationship with them, I liked them and could trust them. So I decided to buy my new guitar from them and ever since I've been subscribed to their channel and regularly watch their videos. When I want some more music equipment who do you think is going to come first to my mind?

Gary Vaynerchuk is one of the early pioneers on YouTube and probably one of the best examples of relationship marketing. Before he became a social media and marketing guru he worked for his Father's wine company. He started a channel called wine library that managed to take his father's company to a $50 million a year business. He would do a show where he tasted and reviewed wine then based on his recommendation people would go to his website and buy his wine. He talks about the early days when he was doing the shows which only got a couple of views for years and says he could so easily have given up. But he persisted and it paid off in a big way. Gary is a great example of focusing on the relationship not an initial sale. His book "Jab Jab Right Hook" talks about how in a social world you need to keep jabbing before you can try and land a right hook. He's basically saying you need to develop the relationship before you go for the right hook - the sale.

The Key

Lead generation is the key to attraction marketing and an educated prospect who already knows, likes, and trusts you is a lot easier to sell to.

Did you know that:

2% of sales are made on the first contact

3% of sales are made on the second contact

5% of sales are made on the third contact

10% of sales are made on the fourth contact

80% of sales are made on the fifth to twelfth contact?

This demonstrates so powerfully my point that you must focus on building a relationship as it might take you ten contacts with a prospect before they'll buy from you.

Lead generation is when you gain a prospect's contact details such as an email address, and phone number in exchange for some kind of value. This can be gained through online, phone, visits and so on. In fact, in every kind of contact you have with a prospect you want to gather as much information as you can from them. In the next chapter I talk about your "Bait" and the type of value you should be giving. Once you're armed with this information you'll be able to follow them up. Remember, persistency is key, seeing as 80% of sales are made on the fifth to twelfth contact. The money is in the follow up. I see so many businesses that are literally losing thousands in revenue by not following up enough. I've devoted a whole chapter to follow up in this book as it's that important.

When you've got their information they are now ready to join your list and you can start the follow up process. Remember people who are a lead might not be ready to buy; they might buy six months from now but the key is you've got their information to keep following them up. That's why you want to be spending your marketing budget on lead generation so you essentially then own that lead and the potential to sell to them as many times as you want. In all of the marketing I created in our training businesses I only focused on lead generation because I knew that going for the initial sale was exactly like everyone else and it completely alienated our target market. I've learnt over the years that if everyone starts doing something I'm doing the complete opposite. I managed to get leads, build a relationship with people and then sell to them over and over again. You all of a sudden go from scratching around for work to having a reliable system that'll take away the pain of knowing where the next customer is going to come from.

CHAPTER 6: YOUR LEAD MAGNET

In the last chapter we stressed the importance of building a relationship and not going for the initial sale. We looked at lead generation as an important initial phase in this process. In this chapter I'm going to be helping you to get going with developing your attraction strategy that you'll present to your target market. It'll be an attraction strategy that'll build value and will be the start of your relationship. This is when the art of attraction marketing takes place. This is where you concentrate on getting leads in exchange for contact details and value. You're no longer the annoying pest trying to sell something, you're welcoming and attracting people towards your business. People are raising their hand and saying those magic words: "Yes, I'm interested".

For me learning about attraction marketing was a turning point in our business and you'll be able to see that this is a much better way to build a sustainable business than bombarding people with your messages like your competitors are no doubt doing. The beauty of attraction marketing is once it's tested and producing results it can be left to run. Yes, you can literally be generating leads as you sleep and with the right systems in place go one step further and start generating income as you sleep.

When I think about generating money while you sleep I always think of the following quote:

"If you don't find a way to make money while you sleep, you will work until you die".

That's exactly why you want to build scalable systems in your business that can be left to run on autopilot and that's what attraction marketing does for you. People come to you. It's scalable and in time can be systemised giving you the freedom to do the things you want to do in life. This will mean that you're not constantly scratching around for the next sale. For me and our business it was a complete turning point, with the sleepless nights of worrying where your next customer is coming from suddenly fading away as you know you've got a way to attract leads and sales into your business. Consistently.

Once you're armed with your lead magnet (a report, a book, a sample etc) you can go out into your market place and start driving traffic. In a later chapter I'll show you how to drive traffic but for now I just want you to focus on building and developing your lead magnet.

Your lead magnet is something that is in most cases free or free plus shipping (to cover costs). This is because of two reasons: The first reason is that free means no risk and the second reason is that we humans can't resist the word 'free'. You see every purchase that we make has some kind of risk factor attached to it like 'what if it doesn't work', 'what if it breaks', and so the list goes on and on. People love free and it gets their attention, I'm sure you've seen free trials and free samples everywhere.

There is also some really cool psychology that works when you are offering your lead magnet for free. Your target market actually raises their hands and say 'yes I'm interested in this' so you're attracting them to you instead of forcing something on them. Even more importantly, once someone says yes to you it's much easier to get them to say yes again. And then again. And again! Because from then on you can gather momentum. You get them to say yes to a small thing, and then they are much more likely to say yes to a larger thing later. The free plus shipping is really important to cover the costs of printing your book, report, product, and of course the shipping. So you'll want to charge a free plus shipping price that can accommodate those costs. It's also powerful because they've actually got to get their credit card out so the relationship has already changed because they're actually giving you money. If you're not sure what would work best for your target market you'll want to split test these two against each other to see what converts the best: Free or free plus shipping.

The Big Secret

With your lead magnet you can apply a big secret to increase scarcity and that involves attaching a price to it and saying it's free but for a limited time only. By attaching a price it increases the value of your offering and it will increase conversions. Of course you must do this in an ethical and genuine way. All it involves is working out the true value of the thing you are giving away and add that price to it. People will then be able to see the true value. With limited offer availability it is also important to make sure you stick to the amount/timescale you are promising.

When it comes to developing your lead magnet you have a whole bunch of different things you can offer. The key to developing your magnet is really getting inside your prospect's mind and finding out as much as you can about them so you know them really well. In Chapter two we covered the importance of knowing your customer so you should by now have a good understanding of what your customer really wants. Based on that you'll be able to create an irresistible offer for your lead magnet. What is it they really want and desire? You never want to give them what they need, you want to give them what they want. If you don't already have some kind of lead magnet then this could literally change your business forever. About 20% of the clients that I work with have some kind of free offer that does at the basic level work as lead generation but doesn't have all the processes in place.

There are many kinds of lead magnets and you can use multiple ones in your business but for now I want to concentrate on two very important lead magnets that I think every single business should have and that is a report or a book. I'm not talking about a best-selling book or a book that is hundreds of pages long. I'm talking about a useful resource that you can put together over a few weeks, sharing some of your expertise.

So why a book? A book is the most powerful way to establish authority, full stop! Now before you think that you can't write a book because of the business you're in, pause and reflect for a moment. Don't fall into the trap of thinking: "I run a bike shop, a music store, I'm a Lawyer, Dentist, Estate Agent, Plumber, Landscaper, Insurance Broker, Website Designer, Yoga Instructor, Trainer, Personal Trainer, so I can't write a book, it's not relevant. I can tell you now that for every kind of business there is you can write a book. There's a million different types of books you can write and you don't even have to write it all yourself; you can give a summary to a ghost writer who will do it all for you. All that matters is to have a book as the most powerful weapon for establishing authority in your market place. I can tell you you'll be the only personal trainer, dentist or plumber etc in town with a book and you'll be positioned completely differently to everyone else. How many business owners do you know that have their own book? And also if no one else is doing it, it's good sign not a bad one! Who are the kind of people that write books? Experts and Celebrities. Just think of it. That's the most important positioning you can have to have influencing power in your market place. Why have I written this book? To establish myself as an authority on marketing. Even if people don't read your book the psychological fact you've written a book will still position you as an expert and authority and it will boost your confidence levels no end.

I hope I've sold you on the idea of writing your book as the best lead magnet there is but just in case you don't want to do that, don't worry. I can appreciate a lot of people won't implement and do that, so what's the next best thing? Well a report has been used for years and years and always works. Usually around 6-12 pages long, a report delivers high value, establishes you as an authority on the subject and solves a specific problem that your potential customer is facing. For our training consultancy we have reports on every single course that we run and it immediately establishes us as an authority on the subjects. Once the potential lead has downloaded the report they then enter our follow up sequence and we may well offer a low ticket item first or pivot to the offer of running an in-house course for them. Think about your business and the problems you solve. Figure out the biggest problem for your potential customers and share your unique solution in the form of an initial lead magnet. The idea is that it's easy to consume this and they can usually read it all as soon as they receive it. When you think of your report you want to think of a transformational result it can achieve for them and something that is the first piece of information they need to consume to get from where they are now to where they want to be. It needs to have a killer title so it grabs your target by the throat. Think of titles like "Finally, sleep well, every night and feel 10 years younger every day". That grabs someone by the throat who's been experiencing sleeping problems. Don't hold back either; it's really important that you deliver such high value because this is the entry point and once you've got them as a lead you can continue to follow them up. You're informing your prospect, educating them, and building a relationship so don't hold back. You're removing the buying fear they experience from most businesses and turning them into an educated buyer who will trust you.

Your report or book should be printed and you can get this done very cheaply from self-publishing book companies, or a local printer if it's for your report. You can also get a professional cover image designer on www.Fivver.com. You want your book in a hard copy format so that you can mail it to them and have their mailing address to follow up with. People may well argue that it's too much of a barrier for your prospects to go through to give away their address, but research shows that someone who is willing to give away their details will be worth a lot more than someone who just gives you their email. With their direct mail address you can send great follow up material that you can't do via email. People like to have physical products they can handle and that's what hard copy reports and books provide.

Just remember that 'free' attracts people if you know where your prospects are and have the right message that makes them put their hand up and say 'Yes I'm interested'. You'll be generating leads that are attracted to you and what you have to offer.

You can have multiple lead magnets to attract prospects but to start with the report or a book will work.

Here's that list as a reminder of other types of lead magnets you can offer for free to your prospects to get them to put their hand up and say "Yes I'm interested":

Webinar

DVD

Products (If you sell suits you could offer free ties or cuff links)

CD

Whitepaper

Trial

Guide

Case Study

Taster Session

Coupon

Newsletter

Demonstration

Tool Kit

Templates

Package

Consultation

Prize draw

Survey

Discount

Training session

Consumer awareness guide

The sole purpose of your lead magnet is to get people to put their hand up and for you to generate a lead. So think of ways to make it sexy, grab people by the throat, unique and don't make it boring. If you're going start with a report the same thing applies: make it attention grabbing and not boring.

It was interesting, when I brought my new BMW the other week I noticed they use similar principles to those I'm explaining here to try and sell me their car insurance. So you buy your BMW and sign all the paperwork. Once that's done you then enter their what in marketing terms we call the 'backend' of the sales funnel. A backend is all the stuff you can sell someone once they've become a customer. And by the way this is where the serious profit sleeps, selling more stuff to existing customers. So I got pitched on all the service packages, tyre insurance, alloy insurance etc. They then pitched me something that got my interest, 7 days free complimentary insurance. They didn't just pitch me insurance, they gave me free insurance for a week. Of course I took them up on the offer, it was low risk, it gave me 7 days to sort out what I'd like to do.

They'd also got my details now so they could put me through their follow up process, which of course was selling me a year's cover. BMW gave me an information pack called "Five questions to ask your insurer". They were making me a more educated prospect when it came to buying my insurance and choosing who I'd like to go with. It really did build a good foundation and a good relationship. Although they could have done a whole host of additional things, at least they kind of got it. It built trust and wasn't bad. I of course got the follow up phone call and emails to sell me on taking a year's cover. I'd have taken the cover but it turns out they wouldn't insure the type of BMW because of my age and that it was too high risk. Here's just a quick example of how even BMW haven't, in my view, got the marketing totally right yet! So, to summarise, get the point that you can't just pitch someone, you've got to educate them, have a low barrier to entry and turn the sales radar off to make the point of sale a lot easier.

Here are some examples of lead magnets used to get prospects to put their hand up and generate leads.

Schedule your consultation now

Just fill out the form below, click the button and we'll get right back to you.
Or if you prefer, call us at (800) 682-0882 . We look forward to hearing from you.

Your Name *	Your Position
Your Email Address *	Your Phone Number
Your Company	Your Company's Location
Subject Area — Other Courses ▼	Level of Training — Multiple Levels ▼
Number of Students	

☐ Yes, I'd also like a free PDF download on ExcelHelp's services

Rather send us an email? No problem. Just email training@excelhelp.com.

REQUEST FREE CONSULTATION NOW ➡

GAIN A COMPETITIVE EDGE WITH SUMTOTAL LEARNING SOLUTIONS

Watch our FREE demo video and take learning to the next level

Leading organisations know that learning and collaboration drive innovation, giving them a competitive advantage.

Get a closer look at the personalised, contextual solutions that have made SumTotal #1 in learning, providing almost 45 million users access to world-class formal training and certification programs.

Fill out the form NOW to watch the demo!

SumTotal Systems uses the information you provide to deliver a customised experience. We do not sell, rent, or loan your personal information to others.

JOIN THE LUCKY LIST AND

ENJOY 20% OFF

Sign up for Lucky emails today
and receive exclusive offers and styles
updates direct to your inbox!

* REQUIRED FIELD

FIRST NAME *

LAST NAME *

EMAIL *

ZIP CODE *

YES! SEND ME UPDATES ON LUCKY KIDS

YES! SEND ME UPDATES ON LUCKY PLUS

SUBMIT

ALREADY A MEMBER? SIGN IN

"Get FREE Cheat Sheet:
"Highest Converting Webinar Registration Schedule" to Learn the Exact Schedule to Register the Most People Possible"

Get the largest conversion possible on your
webinar registration pages with this cheat
sheet

Instant Access

Get My Free Cheat Sheet Now!

No, thanks, I'll pass this opportunity. Take me to the site now...

What's Your Marketing IQ?

When it comes to marketing, are you more like Einstein or a caveman? Or are you somewhere in the middle? It's time you find out where you (and your marketing) stand.

Take the Marketing IQ Test Now

As the owner of a growing business, it's rare that you get a chance to come up for air. And when you do, **there are undoubtedly a million questions on your mind:**

- How well is your business performing?
- What is your competition doing?
- Are there opportunities you're missing?
- How can you make more sales without working more hours?
- What are the latest trends in marketing and sales?

If you've been asking yourself any of these questions, then it's time to take our Marketing IQ test. The test and the results are free.

The IQ Test only takes about 5 minutes to complete, and you'll receive your score as soon as you're finished. It's that easy.

Take your IQ test now!

"I have no special talent. I am only passionately curious."
— Albert Einstein

"Rock. Market. Ting uhg whong uh?"
— Caveman

The exact layout of what goes into making a six-figure income blogging.

This is a full 53-page report, along with an audio MP3 version (listening time 1hr:21m).

Downloaded and read by thousands over the last 6 years.

Download Now!

Get My Free Report Now!

Here's a few examples of direct mail lead generation offers:

PROTYRE
www.protyre.co.uk

The local garage you can TRUST

Unit 1, Westside Centre, Stanway,
Colchester CO3 8PH

01206 934258

Dear Mr Jenkins

FREE Tyre Safety Check

With Easter road trips and unpredictable conditions on the way, drivers need as much grip as possible to stay safe. Only fresh tyres and good tread depth will deliver the best available traction. New tread design, combined with recent rubber compound development can help save fuel too.

So now is the ideal time to pop in for a **FREE tyre safety check** and ensure your tyres are up to the job.

It's a quick and easy check that includes the following:

1. General tyre condition
2. Tread depth
3. Tyre pressures
4. Uneven wear
5. Tyre age

Save money with Goodyear tyres

Once the check is completed our expert technicians will get you safely back on the road in no time. However, should you need some fresh tyres before we say goodbye, we have teamed up with Goodyear to save you **£20 off 4 tyres** or £10 off 2. *Simply bring this letter with you to claim your discount.*

Happy customers enjoy superior service

You will be pleased to hear Protyre consistently score **98% Customer Satisfaction**, when monitored by the Motor Industry Codes of Practice, (backed by Trading Standards). Protyre also have an **Excellent 98% Service Rating** on Feefo – the global feedback engine. But don't take my word for it, turn over and see some recent customer feedback, or visit our website **www.protyre.co.uk** to read more great reviews.

The local garage you can trust

We are also TyreSafe Retailer of the year, proving that we really are the local garage you can trust to look after your vehicle, your pocket, and your safety, all year round.

Yours sincerely

Stephen Brown

Stephen Brown
Centre Manager

P.S. Cut your cost of motoring and experience our superior service for yourself. Call in or book today for your FREE tyre safety check and save £20 when you buy 4 Goodyear Tyres or £10 off 2.

Book your free tyre check www.protyre.co.uk/freetyrecheck

Calls may be recorded for training and monitoring purposes. If you would like to unsubscribe please email us your name and address to unsubscribe@protyre.co.uk

GOODYEAR

£20 off 4 tyres

HOW TO FIND US

Drop into:
Unit 1, Westside Centre,
Stanway, Colchester CO3 8PH

Opening times:
Mon to Fri: 8.30 - 17.30
Saturday: 8.30 - 17.00

Call us on 01206 934258

Order online for same day
fitting at www.protyre.co.uk

MOTOR INDUSTRY
CODE OF PRACTICE
Service and Repair

APPROVED CODE

TyreSafe
TYRE RETAILER
AWARDS WINNER

Do You Know What Your Neighbors at 1234 Main Street Did Last Night?

It May Come As a Surprise to You - But They Have Been Plotting for a Long Time!

Your Neighbors have decided to sell their home and they listed it with Sally Agent of Results Realty.

Now that they've made the decision to sell, they need your help to do it.

Their house is a 3 Bedroom 2 Bath home and it's listed for sale at only $240,000.

To see more pictures and get ALL of the details about this property, visit www.OnlineHouseTours.com and use Tour# 2503230.

If you know anyone who is thinking of buying a home in the CITY area, be sure to tell them about the online tour.

Sally has also prepared a special report called: "The 10 Dumbest Mistakes Smart People Make When Buying or Selling a Home" that we would like to offer to you or anyone you know.

For a FREE copy of this report, visit www.OnlineHouseTours.com/25032 30 or call Sally direct at 555-555-5555.

In the meantime, your neighbors would appreciate it if you kept your eyes and ears open for a buyer for their home!

TAKE THE FREE ONLINE TOUR AT

www.OnlineHouseTours.com/2503230

CHAPTER 7: THE TWO PAGE WEBSITE

When it comes to your website you only really need two pages to promote your lead magnet. These are: a landing page and a thank you page.

Your landing pages are where you send traffic to get people to opt-in and enter their details. This is the most important page because if your landing page is bad you won't convert and you'll be wasting traffic and wasting traffic is not good especially if you're paying for it. The thank you page is where you welcome that new prospect to you and your business. At this point you can start the sales process and maybe offer an upsell but it totally depends on your business. For now you just want to keep it simple and a thank you page is perfect. Now that you've got a new lead your follow up series will start but we will look at that more closely in the next chapter. It's not complicated at all to actually make these pages yourself. You just have to follow my layout and use the software that I'll recommend later.

I want to go into some detail about your website in this chapter so before we look at your landing page and thank you page I want to spend some time talking about this and encouraging you to think carefully about your website as it is at the moment and the changes you may well want to make once you've finished this book. Firstly here is some big news about your website and web designers. Web designers make things look nice, but nice doesn't sell. So when your web designer recommends putting a new fancy slider on your website or a load of design work, remember this: you have 0-8 seconds to make a fantastic impression before your visitor leaves. Now I'm not knocking web designers. In fact I know some amazing web designers who get this whole 8 second rule. To add to the 8 second rule, there's another complexity to consider. Did you know, or have you ever considered this: approximately 96% of visitors that come to your website are not ready to buy. This is massively important. All the more reason to remember the "BUY NOW" doesn't work because it's exactly the same with your website. As with your other lead generation methods, your website also wants to be a lead generating machine with your lead magnet everywhere. If you offer more than one lead magnet which I'm sure you'll have if you offer more than one product or service then you want these on relevant parts of your website, not on the same page. If you're a dog trainer for example specialising in 4 different breeds then each section of your website needs to be broken down into those key categories with your report for each breed at the top...you get the idea. Your main lead magnet, your book, report, dvd, free trial etc must be on your homepage and the first thing that the visitor sees. It needs to be that irresistible offer so that people think they would be mad if they didn't act within that 8 second rule to get it, so they then become a lead. If you're selling ecommerce you'll want to split test lead generation versus an initial sale. Again if you push for the initial sale it may be too much too soon and people won't buy. To some extent with eCommerce it'll depend on the degree of urgency the visitor has and how commoditised your product is. It's usually crazy though to think that you can get people to buy straight away especially if you're not selling ecommerce. Also, here's a tip: ecommerce businesses want to study amazon as they're the biggest online split tester. They keep things boring and simple but in my experience boring and simple works. And Amazon is the proof of that.

Your website MUST have video on it and if you're selling products you must have product demonstration videos on every main product you sell even if they're low quality low budget videos on an iPhone with you reviewing the product. That's better than no video at all.

Everything that you write must convey the benefits of what you sell and you want to study copywriting because the way you can write copy will seriously affect the results you get. Out of all the skills I've learnt I think that being able to write good copy is the most important one I've ever learnt. It takes time and it is very important to collect a swipe file of excellent direct mail from leading experts. I've learnt from the best copywriters in the world and it would be good for you to study them too. Here's a few that you should look at, Dan Kennedy, Joe Sugarman, Gary Halbert, John Calton, Frank Kern and David Olgivy to name but a few. If you don't want to write the copy yourself you can hire a good copywriter. I only ever write copy for a very limited number of clients but a good copywriter like myself won't be cheap. Cheap gets cheap results and who wants cheap results?

Cover your website with social proof and testimonials from people you've worked with and if possible get customer stories on video. Make sure they're real and you don't make fake ones and don't make them look too professional or they could look staged which may create an unauthentic look and feel. As with the product demonstration videos, just an iPhone video will be enough.

Have clear calls to action (CTAs) everywhere on your website to get people to become a lead.

Mobile is now really important so make sure your website is mobile optimised. Videos work best for mobile users as they don't want to scroll through pages and pages of text. You must keep their attention because mobile users are normally on the train, bus, coffee shop, watching TV etc so their attention span isn't the same as if they were sitting at a PC screen.

Your website is very important for people who search your brand but you don't really want to run traffic to your website. Ideally you want to run traffic to your landing page. The only time you really want to drive traffic to your website is if you write a blog or put up a podcast.

Blogging

Blogging is a content marketing tool that is excellent for you to enable to continue your relationship with your prospects and customers. It's the platform that allows you to communicate very effectively but most people do it wrong. I know that in our training business our blogging strategy was initially not getting the results even though the blogs were very good. Some years ago we weren't really clear on the objectives behind the blogs. We were just sharing really well written, expert advice for free. People were then sharing these blogs around their organisation. We know that because sometimes they accidently copied us in on their internal emails and sometimes because they would actually contact us and ask for our permission for them to circulate them internally to their managers etc. We would post the blog and notify our list that this special resource was up on our site. Sometimes it was a written blog and sometimes a video blog. It was easy then to come to the conclusion that blogging doesn't work because all people do is take your free stuff and then not buy. In fact blogging is great to develop a deep relationship with your prospects and customers. It also establishes you more as an authority especially if you are building value and assisting people with helpful articles.

What's more powerful though is to link your blogs to a weekly video show like I showed in the examples in Chapter 3. You can do product reviews and loads of different things. It's really where you bring your personality out as the business owner because people don't follow blogs. They follow people. I could write a whole book about blogging and one of my mentors Dale Partridge is a great person to look at for blogging but for now you want to see it as the platform on which you can communicate with your prospects and customers. It's also a traffic source from which you can get people to sign up for your lead magnet. The way that you can promote your lead magnet is in the side bar of your blog and at the footer of your post. If you are using video blogs you can put this promotion at the bottom of slides you may be showing. This way your readers can see your lead magnet if they've not already signed up for it, and receive it. Things get more complicated and there's a lot more we could consider here if you go on to have multiple lead magnets but for now if you're blogging on your website you want to make sure that your call to action after every post is to get the reader to get their hands on your lead magnet.

You want to use as much video as possible on your website, as I've said and I highly suggest you do a weekly show or podcast and promote that via your blog. In your weekly show you'll build an audience and likely see organic traffic building up. It's also a great way to promote your lead magnet in the show letting people know they can get a free copy of your book or report or whatever it is you're using to attract leads into this system you're building.

You can also get split testing software installed to start testing different lead magnet titles to see what converts better, different colours, video testimonials versus text etc and the list goes on.

The key to unlocking profits from your website is to make sure you clearly have your lead magnet available to generate leads. Otherwise you'll be losing so many visitors who maybe would have become buyers if you're not going for lead generation on your website.

Below are a few examples of lead magnets on blog websites. The meeting report is one from our training consultancy blog:

— Oli Gardner

p.s. If you'd **like to see some brutally honest landing page critiques LIVE!** You should come to the first ever Unbounce Call To Action Conference in Vancouver on September 12th, 2014, where myself and two other conversion rockstars will be looking at landing pages from attendees.

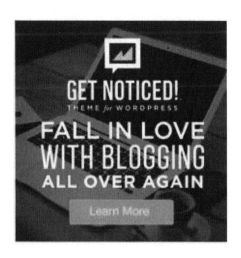

The Landing Page

The landing page is the page that your lead magnet sits on. It's where you gather people's contact information in exchange for your magnet. The way that you gather the information is through your email marketing service provider. Every time someone enters their details they'll automatically get added to your email marketing list and you've now secured their information forever unless they unsubscribe. If you don't know anything about email marketing or have never used it then I suggest you sign up for Mail Chimp or Aweber. They're the cheapest and easiest to use and have very good support. Support is a very important aspect to consider, by the way.

Before you start freaking out like I did when I started doing all this years ago you don't need any technical skills to build these pages. My mentor

Russell Brunson (I'm part of his $25K a year inner circle) has made my life and potentially your life very easy by developing a software called Clickfunnels.

Clickfunnels lets you create these pages very easily and integrates with your email marketing service provider. You don't even need a website so you could just build all your pages in Clickfunnels and it's drag and drop so even my Grandmother could use it! In the examples in Chapter 5 where I talk about lead magnets you can see some of the different types of layouts to use on your landing page. The most important part of any landing page is the headline because that's what will grab attention and get people to put their hand up and say "Yes, I want this." The other great thing about Clickfunnels is you can split test different headlines etc to see which one converts the best.

Don't try and change things that work. I can tell you now that you don't want to experiment with anything else. You must have a headline at the top, video or bullets on the left, and your sign up box on the right. This is what works the best, I've tested it thousands of times and it works the best so don't try and change it up. Below you can see a template for how your landing page should look like.

Landing Page Layout

This is the optimum layout you should choose to use for above the fold.

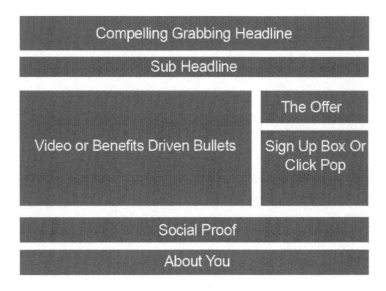

By above the fold I mean what a visitor sees before they have to scroll down on your website or landing page. If you are promoting a report or book then you'll want a well-designed image above the sign up box. On the homepage of your website you also want to follow suit to capture the maximum amount of website traffic you can into leads. This layout example is called a typical "squeeze page" style landing page because it doesn't offer any other option but to enter your contact information or exit. The only link you need to include is a Privacy Policy and any other mandatory pages.

The squeeze page is very simple and here is a quick checklist you can follow with the above template:

A compelling headline

A sub heading

Benefits bullets or a Video

The offer

Call to action (sign up box)

Social Proof

This page is the most important page you'll ever create because that is where you generate your leads. If this fails then everything else won't work because you'll have no leads to try and generate sales from. There are so many factors that go into a good converting landing page. Firstly you want to make sure that what you're offering is something that your target market wants and it's closely linked to what you offer. Remember you're dealing with people on the internet who are scrolling through Facebook, watching cat videos on YouTube, and a whole host of other things, so grabbing attention first through an amazing offer is key. It's what's called a pattern interrupt. The colours and the call to action you have on your submit button all affect your landing page too so the key is to test, test, test! A good landing page should be converting at around 20-30%. How I test my landing pages is to run a 100 visitor test and see what percent of the 100 convert. If it's lower than 10% I know something is wrong and I need to adjust accordingly. The beauty with the landing page is once it's converting at a good rate it just sits there bringing you in new leads for as long as you keep that page up and drive traffic to it. I've got landing pages that I created 3 years ago that are still running and bringing in new leads every week. That's the beauty; once they're running and converting you leave them to run.

If you use Clickfunnels to build your landing page you'll be happy to know that they have proven templates that are already pre-loaded so you just fill in the blanks and edit them. It really makes it easy to create landing pages in a matter of minutes.

You can sign up for a free Clickfunnels account here:

www.clickfunnels.com

Thank you page

Hurrah! You've converted your landing page visitor into a lead but don't excited and forget about everything else because your thank you page is just as important. Your new lead is excited about you because they'll have just taken you up on your lead magnet so you need a great thank you page to reinforce everything. You now have a qualified lead on your hands who, with some guidance, could become a fan or maybe even a lifetime customer.

Everything still counts at this stage so don't let this opportunity go to waste.

Start by actually thanking them for the action they just took and re-emphasise the value of that thing that they've just opted in for. Try and go the extra mile and get them excited so it preframes your lead magnet. What should you do if they've signed up for a consultation or something that needs a human touch to get things rolling? Well you'll want to preframe what's going to happen on the call or the meeting so when the call does happen it causes a trigger in their mind and they already know what to expect.

If you're mailing them stuff in the post you could tease them and tell them you've got some extra special stuff you're going to send as a bonus so it gets them excited to receive your package and they're constantly checking the mail to see if the one from you has arrived yet.

The Truth

Your website is more for your brand presence and for people who search for your business. On its own it's not going to bring you in your fortune. Your funnels may well do so!

CHAPTER 8: THE FOLLOW UP

As business owners it's natural to pour time, money and resources into attracting customers. The truth is many businesses get people to find them online, see an ad, see your sign, walk in your shop, call your office and your receptionist and that's it. There is no capture of name, number, email address, physical address, and no pivot to offer to send an information pack, free report, consultation, nothing! What a waste! I know I've been guilty in the past of this common mistake and I see it happening all the time even as a consumer. If you currently run a business how many wasted leads do you think you've lost? Probably a lot. You'd be surprised and disappointed. I'm sure of that.

You pay the price every time you don't capture information and follow up. Doing nothing once you have received a new lead, enquiry, phone call, every walk-in, is quite frankly like flushing money down the toilet. Imagine you ran an advertising campaign on Google Adwords and you generated

20 leads at a cost of £10 each. If you're not going to do anything with one of those leads you might as well take a crisp £10 note out of your wallet, crumple it up into a ball and flush it down that toilet and watch it go away. If you're going to waste 10 of those then why not get a pile of £10 notes and do it one after the other and see how it feels. Do it now and experience that feeling so you remember each time you fail to follow up a lead it's costing you money each and every time.

The Maths

How would you like to find an extra £60,000 in your business? If you put it to a vote everyone would say 'Yes', and would the future of your business benefit from it? Of course it would. Well, I'm happy to show you where that extra £60,000 is in your business. If you don't already have a business and you're just starting up the key thing to learn here is you must have a follow up system or you'll join the ranks of other businesses who are leaking out so much money due to a lack of follow up. So imagine you spent £1000 to get 50 leads and only 5 leads turned into a meeting and out of those 5 meetings you only closed 2 deals that were worth £1000 each. Well, you've turned £1000 into £2000 which is producing a return, so you carry on repeating that whole process and making a good return. However, consider this: how about the 45 leads who didn't turn up for a meeting, so they've been wasted but they actually had put their hand up and expressed interested in what you can offer. But maybe the timing wasn't right or they didn't couldn't come to a meeting, or join that webinar. Now, imagine if through the correct follow up, the closing rate of meetings rose to 20 meetings and the closing rate of those meetings increased to 10. You've now added an extra £8000 after cost of acquisition to your business. Here's when the maths gets good. If that happened every month for the next 12 months it works out to an extra £96,000! What if you can make just 5 of every 10 new customers refer one new customer through a referral follow up system? That's an extra £5000 that cost you nothing to acquire, just the effort and knowledge to have the right follow up systems in place.

Do you remember the stats?

2% of sales are made on the first contact

3% of sales are made on the second contact

5% of sales are made on the third contact

10% of sales are made on the fourth contact

80% of sales are made on the fifth to twelfth contact.

Did you know that if we can have 8 contacts within a 12 day period from them requesting your lead magnet it can increase the likelihood of getting business by 500%. Most business only try one or two times and then give up.

So, the price is a hefty one to pay if you don't follow up on your leads.

So what does follow up look like?

After your prospect has received your lead magnet it still might not be the right time for them to buy. They might need warming up consistently until the point when they're ready to buy and you've developed the relationship further. It completely depends on what your lead magnet is and what your sales process is but you've got two main options to start with.

You can follow up with an immediate offer or you can continue to provide value and then pivot towards an offer.

Different types of follow up

Email Marketing
Direct Mail
Retargeting
Phone

To get the best result when following up on your leads you want to combine a mix of follow up strategies. To get started I'd suggest email marketing and direct mail as they work very well together. A cheaper way to start with so you keep print costs down would be email marketing and the phone.

Here's an example of the follow up system I implemented into our training consultancy.

Our lead magnet is a free report and that's the start of the whole process. Once they've filled in their email address and name I then ask for shipping details to send a hard copy of the report and some exclusive bonuses. I put this step in after to make sure I get the name and email first. After we've got a new lead the follow up process begins and it's completely automated. We have a member of staff that takes care of sending out the mail, a member of staff who works the phones, and the email follow ups are all programmed in an autoresponder to go out in a certain order. This is why I love attraction marketing and this simple formula because once it's in place it can be left to run.

In the follow up process our offer is to run the course they've downloaded a report about, in-house to their members of staff. It's quite a long sales process so the whole follow up process is about getting them on the phone and closing them on the training. You can see in our follow up we don't pitch running the course straight away. I start by building more value first. However in the free report there is always a call to action to call us or email us if they'd like to run the course in house. Every piece of material you give any prospect should always include a call to action with your details. If they do decide they want to get in touch to see how you can help them further they will be able to.

All the following emails have a P.S at the bottom with a clear call to action saying - If you're looking to speak to us about running this course in-house, please simply reply to this email or call 0845 XXX XXX. It's not directly asking for the sale, it's just reminding them that the next step should be to talk to us.

Email Follow Up Sequence

Immediately – Here's an example from our training business: Thank you for requesting your free repot on "How to chair effective meetings that produce results". This email includes a PDF download link for immediate access, instructions on what's going to happen next with a hard copy being sent to them and what they can expect from us moving forward, and then finally a welcome video from our Chief Executive informing the new lead all about our business and how we can help them.

Day 2 - On day two we send out an email that re-emphasises the report with a reminder of the download link as we want them to consume the information as it establishes our company as an authority on the subject. We also let them know that we've recorded a new video especially for them and it will be released over the next few days.

Day 4 - We send out the pre-recorded video that is a 20 minute presentation giving a snapshot of the course and the key learning points that delegates will learn on our chairing meetings training course. At the end of the video we then pitch on getting in touch to discuss running the course in-house. This is where most of our sales come from because we're actually demonstrating how much of an authority we are on the subject by giving them a video taster of how the course will run. We are providing so much value and all our clients comment on how good our videos are and how it was a turning point in their decision. We're showing we're the best.

Day 7 - The last three emails have all provided good will and value. We've not just continuously been pitching for the sale but of course there has to be a transition to a full on pitch. So on day 7 I send out an email that is basically a sales letter trying to get them to go ahead and book the training course.

Day 12 - On day twelve I send a video testimonial about the course and again a sales letter email pitching the course.

Day 14 - I send out a blog post about the topic, chairing meetings and at the bottom of the blog the call to action is to book the in-house course and get in touch. Remember all of these emails have a P.S trying to get them to either email back or call us up.

Day 17 - You can't keep going on about this

subject because their behaviour shows you that for whatever reason they're not interested. It's now time to segment them onto another topic of piece of content. This is called behavioural response email marketing and is a very advanced email marketing strategy that I can't go into detail about now. If you'd like know how to transplant all of this into your business then you can apply to work with me 1-1. I only work with a handful of clients each month; however you can email my team and see if there are any available slots: support@alexjenkins.org

Direct Mail Follow Up Sequence

Here's an example :

Day 3 - A bonus package that along with the report contains all other kinds of information related to the subject is sent out by us. This is called a 'shock and awe' package because you shock the prospect with so much cool information. Lots of different things go into this package but the main thing is a full sales letter selling the course related to the free report they requested.

Day 6 - A postcard that reminds them about the sales letter that was sent out and that they should speak to us about running the course in-house. The postcard also resells the course and the benefits it will provide to them.

Day 9 - We send out a letter that includes a costa coffee card with £5 credit. I won't talk about what goes into the letter but the idea is that they can go and get a drink on us and read through the material we've sent them.

Day 13 - We send out a postcard telling them to go to the web address and watch the 20 minute presentation which we sent out in email number 4. We know from feedback that the video works really well, so we want to make sure they watch it. You could split test by sending out a DVD recording or a CD. We've not done this yet but I'm thinking about split testing to explore further what gets the best result.

So that's the online and offline follow up system we use for all of our courses. We do follow up on the phone as well but that doesn't start until they've received the shock and awe package as it starts the conversation. "Hi Mary, the reason for the call today was because we recently send you X package…"

Once we've got them on the phone and they're going ahead with booking the course, all the follow ups stop automatically and they go onto another list about other products and services that we offer.

If they've gone through our follow up sequence and not bought from us we segment them onto another piece of content but in our CRM we know that they originally expressed interest in our Chairing Meetings Course. So every month we phone up and follow up because it could be 6 months before they buy. Just because they didn't buy through your first stage of follow up doesn't mean they won't buy at all. So they start phase two of follow up where they'll receive a monthly call check in.

For our email marketing we use an advanced email marketing campaign which is called the "are you still". The "are you still" is called a reactivation campaign that simply asks the person "Are you still looking for a chairing meetings training course"? The email is a great way to see if that person is still interested in what caught their eye in the first place. This is a great follow up process you can do right now if you've got a business and you've got the information of people who did not buy from you. Send out and email saying: "Are you still looking for…[insert what you do]". If you've got a contact number, pick up the phone and ask that simple question.

This is just one type of follow up for new leads. Once you have a new customer you want to start different follow up systems for referrals and other products and services that you can offer. This is called the backend but for now to keep it simple you want to create a follow up system for your lead magnet you've created. Once you've got it working and converting you'll then want to create another lead magnet so that you've got multiple ways to attract new people for your different products and services. We have 20 different courses so we need 20 different lead magnets to get super targeted leads.

The beauty of the follow up is that this is where the sale takes place or where the sales process starts. However you never want to underestimate the amount of follow up it can take to generate that next sale. With the correct offer, sales copy, and sales process, you should be generating a good amount of sales because your leads are so well qualified and their sales resistance is low.

The content you send out to your new leads and the way you follow them up is the most vital part of your marketing, as it's potentially what makes the sale.

Make sure your follow up is persuasive, interesting, and creative. Put yourself in the customer's shoes and research how to write good influencing copy that gets people to take action because that's the sole purpose of your follow up. What's going to push their buttons and get them to respond? Go back to Chapter 3 and make sure you're tailoring your follow up series and copy to your audience.

CHAPTER 9: TRAFFIC SOURCES & PAID ADVERTISING

It might seem like we've worked backwards because actually it all starts with driving traffic to your lead magnet but I wanted to leave traffic until now. The reason is everything we've done up until now is the system. You should now have built the foundations for attracting new leads and sales. You know your target market, you know where they're hanging out, you've got a lead magnet that's your piece of bait to lure them in, and you've got your follow up sequence to turn those new leads into sales. It's now time to fill the system with traffic.

When it comes to traffic you've got three types of traffic.

Traffic that you own

Traffic that you pay for

Traffic that is organic

Traffic that you own

The best type of traffic is the traffic that you own and it's the most important. It's your email list that you've built, your direct mail list, your social media followers, blog post readers, etc. The reason why you're in a position to own this traffic is because you can send out an email, post a message to your followers and you'll generate instant traffic and you can send that traffic to anywhere you want. You don't have to go to Google or Facebook to buy traffic or do anything else except turn to your list. That's why it's so important to build a list through attraction marketing and lead magnets. Your list is your asset that'll drive your business for years to come. That's why you want to build a good lasting relationship with your leads and customers on your list because when you want to send out a marketing message you don't need to pay for any marketing costs because you've already acquired them and they're on your list. When you sell to your list over and over again it's pure profit with no costs to generate the sale. The biggest goal you should have in your business is to build a massive list that you can go to at any time to generate sales and you'll do that through the attraction marketing formula.

I'd also put referrals in this category because you can directly ask your existing customers to refer someone and therefore that traffic has come to you from traffic you own.

Traffic that you pay for

This is the second best type of traffic because you can buy it and tell it where to go. When someone clicks on your ad you have the ability to send those clicks to anywhere you want. This does not just include online traffic. If you know that your target market read a certain magazine etc then you can display an ad in the magazine to go to a website page or call a number to get your lead magnet. If you buy a direct mail list of men over 40 who play golf you can send a direct mail campaign and drive the traffic to your lead magnet the same way. If you know where your traffic is then you'll have to pay for it; it doesn't just magically turn up until you've built a big enough list.

Here's a few examples of traffic below that you can buy within the context of a direct response based ad that triggers immediate action to take you up on your lead magnet.

List rental (pay to use other people's lists)
Pay-per-click ads (Facebook, Google, Yahoo etc)
Native ads
Affiliates and joint ventures
Banner ads
TV
Radio
Magazines
Newspapers

Direct Mail

The whole objective behind traffic you pay for is to generate leads and build a list that you create goodwill with, a relationship, so you can sell as many products and services as you wish. Imagine sending traffic that you have to buy straight to a sales offer. Your conversion rate would be around 1-3% and you'd have built no list. That's why you must focus on sending paid traffic to your lead magnet and building a list.

Traffic that is organic

Traffic that you get organically you can't control because it just shows up, so if someone see my name on Facebook, googles me and lands on a random page on my website, I've had no control over that process. There are lots of different types of organic traffic. It could be as simple as a word of mouth recommendation. You won't know how they got to your website or how they found your phone number, so all you want to do is make sure lead generation is key on your website and if someone randomly phones up you get their contact information right away. You want to turn the traffic that is organic into traffic that you own.

Paid Advertising

The first goal of paid advertising is to generate leads and build your list. But the second goal that is just as important as the first is to make paid advertising profitable and to get a return on your investment. You can't just keep building a list and generating leads at a cost with no sales process and no return. That's why in the follow up process you need to ask for the sale and generate new customers after you've built value and they can trust you. Paid advertising works really well when you work out your cost per lead. So for example if you get 100 leads for an ad spend of £1000, your cost per lead is £10. If you're selling a product that costs £500 you only need to get two sales out of 100 to break even and any more is all profit. But don't forget you've still got 98 leads to follow up with and they're now on your list and traffic that you control.

The only time I will ever send paid advertising to an immediate offer is if that person is searching for the exact product or service I can offer and is highly likely to buy.

I will only ever send paid traffic if I know they're really hot leads and likely to convert. However, don't forget that the landing page I send people to will have a report on the page to help generate leads but the main call to action is sign up for this course.

Here's an example below from my Google Adwords account and the keyword was on exact match so I knew that they were really hot leads coming to our landing page looking for our course. I tested this for a couple of weeks but I know the conversion rate could have been higher because half of the people were looking for an open course not an in-house course but we rarely run open courses anymore so I just wanted in-house training results. The profit margin is also higher on in-house courses. Now I share this example below because it's a great way of investing money to get a load more back. As you can see below my ad spend was £192.82 and I'd set up google conversion so I knew my conversion rate. We got 2 conversions and each conversion was worth £1500. So for a spend of £192.82 I produced a return of £2,807.18. Pretty good return on investment wouldn't you say? Now I'm going to put in a disclaimer here by saying my results aren't typical and I'm not saying that you can get the same results. All I'm showing is what's worked in my business.

That would be the only time you'd run paid traffic

to an immediate offer because the conversion rates are usually very low especially from cold traffic. So all your other paid advertising campaigns need to promote your lead magnet and generate leads.

At the moment Facebook advertising is really the big breakthrough for business owners. If your target market are on Facebook you must use Facebook advertising to drive people towards your lead magnet. You can display a laser precise ad right in front of your perfect prospect. They've got such great targeting features and you can get a very low cost per click.

You want to find the paid traffic source that works best for your target market. If they're not on Twitter, don't use Twitter. If they don't read your trade magazine don't advertise in it. Only use the traffic source that has your target market in it. It's quite straightforward at the end of the day. You want to start with a low budget and test the water before you dive straight in spending money and not seeing a return or not having the right process in place from the start.

Every piece of traffic that you get you want to promote your lead magnet to at all times. So your social media posts should promote and link to your lead magnet. Your YouTube videos should promote your lead magnet. Don't purely link to your website, that's just a waste of a lead. Your blogs should promote your lead magnets, your newsletter that you send out every month should include lead magnets, in fact every piece of marketing content you produce should include a lead magnet and a clear call to action. Remember that.

Never just go for an initial sale when you're paying for traffic because you're wasting leads and not building a list.

The key is to put the right message in front of the right market so make sure you do your research to find out where you can buy traffic from.

Below I will share with you some examples of Facebook and Google Adwords pay-per-click to give you an idea of what the ads look like.

Facebook Pay-Per-Click Examples

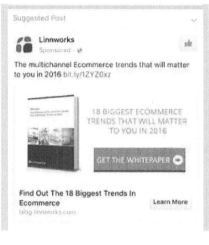

Facebook is the perfect place to start when it comes to running paid advertising to generate new leads. You can target and display an ad to your exact target market. Below is an example of how I target Dentists with a lead magnet offer through Facebook. You can see in the targeting section how precise it is in finding Dentists on Facebook. On the right you can see that my potential reach is 3,900 people in the UK.

Google Adwords Pay-Per-Click

Google and Facebook are both great places to start when running paid online advertising. It all comes back to Chapter 3 and knowing your customer. Once you know your customer and where they hang out, you can put your lead magnet as a piece of bait right in front of their nose. I could write a whole book about running different types of traffic to your lead magnet but for now I just want you to absolutely understand that you have three types of traffic to run to your lead magnet, traffic that you own, traffic that you pay for, and traffic that is organic.

If you already have a list of leads on an email database then you'll want to develop your lead magnet and send them directly to it. If they take you up on your lead magnet then they'll start the whole system and could become buyers not just leads.

The next best step would be to see if your prospects are actively searching keywords around what you do and start split testing some ads on a very low budget. A quick warning about Google Adwords,: the settings that come as standard when you get an account and set up ads are actually going to burn through your budget. This is because the keyword match type is set to broad match on the standard setting. This means that if your keyword is "Personal Trainer Essex" your ad will appear for any one of those words. So if someone searches Essex your ad will appear and if people who are not relevant are clicking on your ad you'll be flushing your money down the toilet. Again! When I first started doing Google Adwords I just dived in straight away without actually taking the time to learn from the best and I did exactly that. I wasted so much money, got no results, and then blamed Google Adwords. "It was all their fault" I said. " It doesn't work" I moaned. Actually the reality was I didn't know how to use it. I can now say that I've mastered it and generated thousands of pounds with a great return on investment.

So remember when it comes to Adwords you want to change the match type from broad match to exact or phrase match and that is under the keyword settings. This tip alone is worth you reading this book as 99% of people don't know this and burn through so much wasted ad spend it's crazy.

Another quick tip with Adwords is that you only want to be positioned in the top four on the first page. There are many factors for getting to be in the top positions. These include the amount you bid per click, your page quality score, your click through rate, etc but you must be in the top four to get the best results. You can also make your ad bigger with site extensions, call outs, and other very clever things to make your ad twice as big as anyone else. Again this is advanced stuff that your competitors won't know about.

Facebook is a gold mine at the moment and I personally know people generating thousands of leads every day from Facebook. Have you ever noticed if you've got a Facebook account they always prompt you to fill out your job title and other things about you? They do this for one reason, and that one reason is so that people like me can find you better on Facebook and display ads in front of you. Facebook makes its money from marketeers spending money on advertising, so it makes sense for Facebook to make sure they've got our target market in their system. You can target so specifically because Facebook knows what you like, what you comment on, what fan pages you like, which websites you've clicked on, your marital status, your income, your job title, etc. They know more than you can even begin to imagine and it's quite scary when you think about it. It's also the perfect weapon for us to deliver a lead magnet offer in front of our target market and get our potential customers in our sales funnel isn't it?

All your social media profiles are a traffic system so start writing engaging posts that lead someone to your lead magnet. Start thinking of posts you can put up and organise to go out automatically. You can use Hootsuite to do this.

If you're in B2B, LinkedIn is a great tool for driving traffic but I get bombarded by people every day in my inbox and it's the same old pitch every time. No one has ever said to me… "Hi Alex, I've got this awesome (lead magnet) for you and I want you to have it for free. It's going to do XYZ for you and it's full of awesome stuff. It's going to really help you achieve X. Simply go here to get a copy." See how different that kind of message is to someone? Do you think that would get someone's attention? Of course it would, you're not like everyone else who is giving the same pitch over and over again. You can see how the attraction marketing formula works, you're delivering value to people and attracting them to you. In the example above you can get that person off LinkedIn and into your system and now you have them as a lead to follow up in whatever follow up sequence you want. You now control the situation.

LinkedIn is also great for content marketing and

you can use LinkedIn Pulse to write posts. You can see below a post we produced in our training consultancy and it received 3,341 views with 259 likes. What do you think was at the end of this post? You guessed it. It was a call to action to get our lead magnet that was a report all about recruiting staff. It produced 150 leads and 8 new clients straight off the bat, but remember we built an asset of 150 leads that we now own and can market to them over and over again.

How to recruit and select the best person for the job

Sep 20, 2014 | 3,341 views △ 259 Likes ⊂⊃ 26 Comments | ⊞ ▣ ▢

Begin with the end in mind – how to recruit/select the best person for the job

You've probably heard the expression before 'Fail to prepare and you will be preparing to fail'. At no time is this more true than when you are looking to appoint a new person to your team. Get this wrong and you will experience a host of problems. You risk destabilising a previously cohesive, high performing team, and unless you are familiar with employment legislation, you could end up with all kinds of issues and expenses.

So, get your recruitment process clear to minimise these risks:

1 Don't jump in – do a 'job analysis'

Based on your research as a result of working through Chapter 3 you should have a good understanding of where your prospects and customers hang out and now you should map out your own traffic plan. Think of your traffic as marketing pillars that will hold your lead magnets up with new leads every day. If you only have one traffic pillar and that disappears tomorrow your lead magnet will fall down and your business could go under. Get one working well and then build another, and another, until you've got multiple pillars holding up your lead magnet at the same time.

Imagine that your lead magnet is a roof; only one traffic source is just about holding up although it's almost falling down.

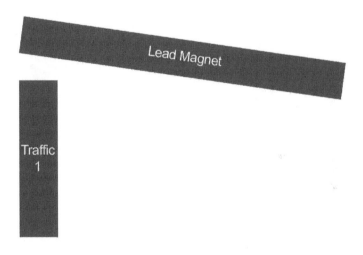

I know people that have had their advertising accounts suspended and their whole business has gone down with it because they relied on one source of traffic.

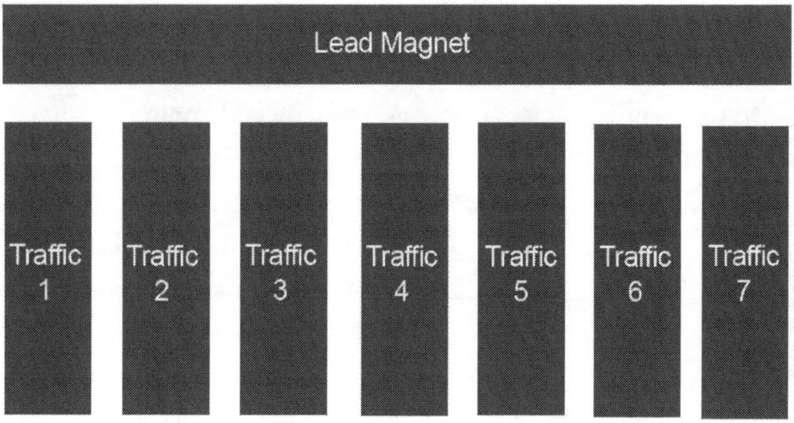
Lead Magnet
Traffic 1
Traffic 2
Traffic 3
Traffic 4
Traffic 5
Traffic 6
Traffic 7

CHAPTER 10: THE HIDDEN PROFITS IN YOUR BUSINESS

The marketing legend Jay Abraham whom I've studied over the years talks about three way to grow a business.

So what are the three ways to grow a business?

1) Increase the number of customers: get more new prospects into paying customers

2) Increase the average transaction: get each customer to buy more at each purchase

3) Increase the frequency that the average customer buys from you: get each customer to buy from you more often

With the art of attraction marketing formula you'll have nailed number 1 because you'll be generating new leads and customers.

The hidden profits in your business lie in number 2: get each new customer to buy more. But before we move on to getting your customers to buy more from you, let's have a quick recap on what you should have achieved so far.

By now you should understand that your marketing needs to be generating leads and a list, not merely pitching people for an initial sale. Once you've generated a lead you then follow up to generate the sale.

Remember, 8 out of 10 small businesses fail and they fail because of a lack of cash flow. You must have a system in place that takes someone that doesn't know you or your business into someone that raises their hand and says "Yes I'm interested". The key to the art of attraction marketing formula is to now have a process to generate new leads and new customers every day.

You should now have a clear understanding of your target market, who your ideal customer is, and where they hang out online and offline.

You should have created a lead magnet that is relevant to your target market to use as your bait to attract people and convert them into leads.

You should have created your landing page and thank you page.

You should have a follow up email marketing

sequence written and/or a phone follow up script or direct mail sequence. I'd also suggest you put a retargeting pixel on your thank you page so you can use retargeting in your follow up too.

You should have a traffic strategy for paid advertising and the traffic that you own.

You should now be testing running traffic in small quantities to test your conversion rate.

Now you have a system that's mostly automated to bring you new leads and customers every day. You just need to keep feeding the system with traffic and split testing different parts of the process to maximise conversions.

Your follow up process should be converting a percentage of your leads into customers, so what's next? Well, you'll want to keep following your leads up with the same offer or segment them onto an alternative lead magnet or offer. But for the people that buy your core offer that you present in your follow up process you want to unlock the hidden profits.

The hidden profits in your business is to sell other products and services to your existing customers. This is called upselling and if you look at most successful businesses they do the same. Back to my story about buying my BMW, once I'd signed the paperwork they then tried up selling additional products and services like tyre insurance, servicing etc. You can even look at McDonalds, because when you buy just a cheeseburger they then try and upsell you on a meal because they know they make more profit selling you a meal instead of a single burger.

I wanted to make this book as simple as possible and it follows a simple proven formula that any business can use.

You drive traffic to a lead magnet that collects leads and you then follow up on those leads. Pretty simple right? It is simple and anyone can implement this into their business and get results. It's a type of funnel and funnels come in many different shapes and sizes. Here's an example of how an upsell funnel would look like. You can see it's the same as the one above but you've got the added step of an upsell.

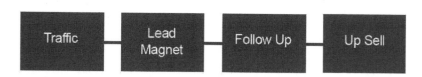

Imagine if 10 new customers brought your product or service each month and only just two of them brought your upsell offer, and that upsell produced an extra £1000 in pure profit. It's pure profit because it's cost you nothing to acquire that extra sale because they're your customers, you've already got them through the door. This also means that in return you can spend more to acquire a lead and a customer than your competitors. When I think of this the famous words from the legend Dan Kennedy come to mind:

"Ultimately, the business that can spend the most to acquire a customer wins."

The more offerings and funnels you can put your customers down, the more each customer will be worth to you. The more your customers are worth to you, the more you can spend to acquire them. Once your customers buy from you, you need to move them into other communication funnels that build a relationship and follow up on another product or service.

There are many different ways to upsell your customers. You could offer premium services, tailored solutions, monthly support, packages, etc. The list goes on and on but the key to remember is that a buyer is a buyer is a buyer. They'll buy from you again so maximise customer value and upsell!

Imagine two business owners, one is called Mark and the other Peter. They both picked a hot market - supplements. Competitive but very profitable if done right. They both sold the same product - a fat loss supplement pill aimed at women over 40 who'd had kids and had struggled ever since to get back to the weight they wanted. Finding time throughout the day to exercise has always been a problem, so a fat burning supplement is the perfect solution.

So Mark and Peter both started to dig around and

look for their target market who were women over 40. They both identified that Facebook advertising was a perfect source for those they wanted to target. They also found through research on Google that the keyword "fat burning pill for older women" had a big search volume. Armed with the right platform to drive traffic from, they knew people were actively looking for the product, so they both decided to run traffic straight to an offer to buy the pills. After three months of testing and running ads, Mark's front end sales had generated £18,800 in revenue. He'd spent £9,400 on advertising, his cost of producing the product was £4000 and his running costs were £2500. So his total profit was £2,900 which is £966.67 a month. His dream of running his own supplement brand was only producing him £966.67 a month, Not even a third of his corporate salary and was struggling to provide for his family. My mentor Com Mirza who is worth $500million+ calls this entrepreneurial suicide. Mark loads up Word on his PC and starts writing his CV again.

Now let's imagine Peter, Peter's front end sales over the three months had generated £15,600 which was less than Mark's turnover. His ad spend was £7,300 and his cost of producing the product was £5,300 and his running costs £2,100. His profit was a disappointing £900! That was only £300 a month but at least he was making a profit. Here's where the big tipping point happens and it all comes down to upselling. Peter had taken time to learn from other successful supplement entrepreneurs, he'd done his research, read books on marketing, got mentors. Peter knew that the profit in his business lay in getting his customers that said yes once to say yes again. So what did he do?

Peter applied an immediate upsell after people had bought to be able to add more bottles to their order. This resulted in a 35% conversion rate. So 35% of people brought more straightaway. He then put all his new customers who didn't buy the upsell into a follow up sequence promoting a monthly subscription. He then joint ventured with a personal trainer to develop a home workout programme and eating plan. All his new customers on his list then got the promotion for the workout programme and eating plan resulting in Peter receiving 60% commission on all sales.

You see with the two examples about how one business failed because Mark didn't implement an upsell process to get his new customers to spend more money. He only concentrated on the front end and ignored the backend. The backend is truly where your profit lies in your business.

CHAPTER 11: CONCLUSION

I'm guessing you're now feeling a bit overwhelmed with what it really takes to build a system that generates leads and sales for your business. You should feel proud of yourself though because you've just read through a high level marketing strategy that could transform your business.

It's a good thing that you're feeling overwhelmed because your brain is starting to make connections and starting to figure out how you can apply this to your business. It's strategizing what type of lead magnet you're going to offer, the type of traffic you're going to send, what your email marketing follow up sequences are going to look like. All this is happening although you might feel overwhelmed.

Your most important takeaway is that from now on you're not going to do any kind of brand building or spending valuable marketing money on pitching for an initial sale. Instead you're going to attract people towards you through your lead magnet and you're going to get people who have raised their hand. It changes the whole relationship and the whole way you do business. You're going to develop lead magnets, generate leads, and generate sales.

Here's what you should do next:

1. Create a USP
2. Decide who your customers are and where they hang out
3. Create a lead magnet
4. Build your follow up sequence
5. Drive traffic

Do those five things before you build your upsells because you want to get this working and converting first. Once you've got the system converting build your upsell and then move on to creating another lead magnet and another system if it's applicable to your business.

Many people who read this book want me to help them personally and to look at their business, identify the holes, and build systems that create dramatic increases in sales and profit.

The beauty of this book and this system is it's quite a simple concept that can double or even triple sales within a few months.

This book is going to be available to everyone who is serious about growing their business so I know it's going to be hard to accommodate everyone who wants more personalised help. So I've created something special for readers of this book and I've opened up my coaching programme so that I can personally help you one on one with your business. I will help you make the changes you need to make in your business to take it to the next level.

If you're interested in me personally working with you every month to help you implement everything, you can apply here:

www.smartbizsecretscoaching.com

or email:

support@smartbizsecrets.com

After you apply, a member of my team will be in touch to see if it's a good fit. If it is then we could actually be spending a day together as soon as next month.

You can also sign up on my blog:

www.smartbizsecrets.com to receive my latest updates.

And with that... will end this book

Thank you so much for reading, and I wish you all the success in your business.

Alex Jenkins

ABOUT THE AUTHOR

Alex Jenkins is an author, entrepreneur, and marketing expert who is a trusted advisor to entrepreneurs and business owners on marketing, internet marketing, and business success.

After running his own successful business, he now shows entrepreneurs and business owners how to grow their business and increase their profits through advanced sales and marketing strategies.

What gives Alex his unique edge is that he's been in the trenches and learnt the hard way. He's actually gone through the ups and downs of running a business and has come out the other end with success. He contributes a lot of this success to finding extremely successful mentors and learning from the best business and marketing minds in the world.

70797850R00081

Made in the USA
Columbia, SC
14 May 2017